H

Readers are requested to keep the Books clean,
to avoid turning down the leaves, and to report
any damage that has not been previously recorded
by the Librarian at the end of the book.

N.B.   No periodical is allowed to be taken out
of the Reading Room.

ISLAND ROAD TO AFRICA

ROGER HIGHAM

ISLAND ROAD
TO AFRICA

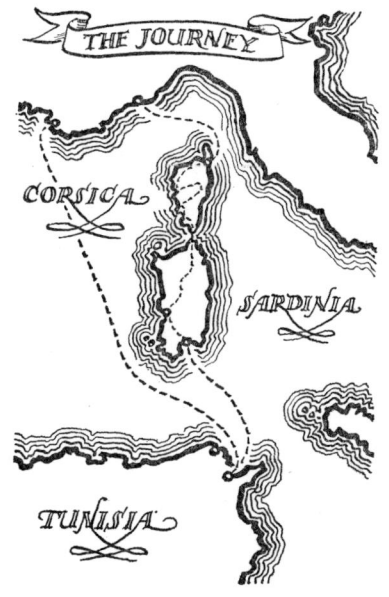

WITH ILLUSTRATIONS BY THE AUTHOR
AND FOUR MAPS

LONDON
J. M. DENT & SONS LTD

© Roger Higham, 1968
All rights reserved
Printed in Great Britain
by
Western Printing Services Ltd, Bristol
for
J. M. DENT & SONS LTD
Aldine House · Bedford Street · London
First published 1968

CONTENTS

∽ 1 ∽
CORSICA

∽ 2 ∽
SARDINIA

∽ 3 ∽
TUNISIA

To H. G. H.

ILLUSTRATIONS

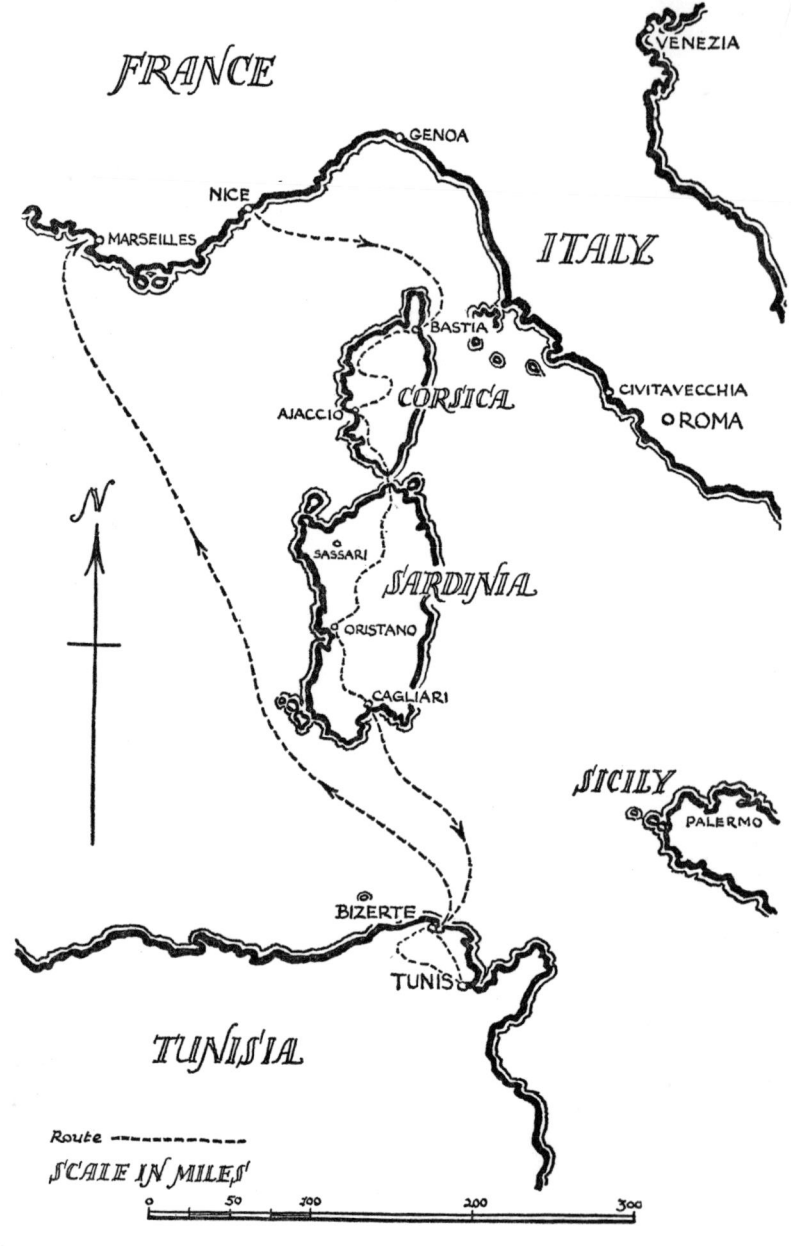

FRANCE

VENEZIA

GENOA

NICE

ITALY

MARSEILLES

BASTIA

CORSICA

CIVITAVECCHIA

AJACCIO

○ ROMA

N

SASSARI

SARDINIA

ORISTANO

CAGLIARI

SICILY

PALERMO

BIZERTE

TUNIS

TUNISIA

Route --------------

SCALE IN MILES

0   50   100   200   300

PART ONE

CORSICA

Chapter One

THE NORTH COAST

A fiery red sun rose from the haze over the yellow oiled-silk Tyrrhenian Sea. Gulls, wearing unaccustomed black, wove angular patterns against it; houses and hotels gleamed palely on the shore and behind them loomed the dark mountains.

At half past seven on a Sunday morning in October, the *Sampiero Corso* docked in Bastia harbour, in North-East Corsica. A small group of handkerchief-wavers on the quayside shouted cheerfully to homecoming friends and relations still aboard. Behind them was the slightly chilling presence of a Foreign Legion sergeant, staring inscrutably straight in front of him. The gangplank was down and the passengers filed ashore. One of them, burdened with a bulging rucksack, was greeted only with a stare or two because he was a stranger and furthermore was dressed like a tramp.

At this point I suppose I shall have to admit to being the aforesaid stranger and therefore the aforesaid tramp.

I hadn't intended to arrive in Bastia on a Sunday morning at all, I wanted to get to Ajaccio on a Friday. Unfortunately in Nice I had discovered that there was no boat to Ajaccio. In fact there was no boat to anywhere until the *Sampiero Corso* sailed, three days later. After that I was glad enough to be in Corsica at all, even if it was Sunday and all the shops were closed and I hadn't any food *and* I had to revise all my plans for the journey *and* I'd spent as much in three days in Nice as I had allowed for a week in Corsica.

From the wharf I drifted along the Place Saint-Nicholas and the Quai des Martyrs de la Liberation: it takes longer to say that than to walk along it as far as the old harbour. This latter was a placid basin, used by fishermen and yachtsmen, surrounded on its landward sides by tall stone houses in varying stages of dilapidation, and a hill on which stood the Citadel. This, a convenient promontory into the sea, consisted of the unadorned and utilitarian walls of a fortress built in the 1400's and the roofs of the houses that had been the nucleus of the town. Opposite this bulk, across the little harbour, the two graceful towers of the church of Saint John the Baptist rose above the rooftops. Apart from an occasional bleary-eyed bar-keeper putting out tables and chairs and sweeping his forecourt, there was no one about; the air was still, the boats motionless at their moorings with reflections as clear as themselves, the washing, strung from house to house in the narrow alleyways, hung limp. The sun, rising a little further, pulled a string of schoolchildren out of the imposing establishment off the Boulevard General Giraud and sent them clattering along the pavements to church.

I didn't feel inclined to hang around in Bastia waiting for something to happen, because Bastia on a Sunday morning had that feeling that nothing ever would. I found a baker's shop open in the Boulevard General Giraud, bought fourteen inches of bread and departed up the hill and out of the town. Within half an hour I had left behind all the fancy villas, gained a couple of hundred feet and begun to sweat profusely. A pause for the removal of certain garments and the intake of what breakfast I could summon up, and I was off again, greeting on the way a nice old lady in black who offered me the unsolicited information that there was a bus-stop just up the road.

The road was apparently going to wind uphill all the way until it reached a certain Col de Teghime, whereon it would wind all the way down again. This kind of thing I soon discovered was the standard behaviour of all roads in Corsica. This one now ran along the edge of the mountain it was climbing, affording excellent views over its deep and savage defiles dropping away to the coastal plain, Bastia, and the distant shining waters of a shallow lake called Etang de Biguglia. Nearer at hand the terrain consisted of rough, tussocky grass and vast areas of evergreen scrub. This, an extraordinary mixture of, to me, unidentifiable bushes and shrubs, was called the maquis, and it appeared to cover a remarkably large part of Corsica's surface area. One of its constituent bushes sported some appetising looking red berries, big as cherries but softer in texture and knobbly in appearance. For all I knew they might be as beneficial to the health as Deadly Nightshade, so I gave them a wide berth until I knew more about them. Curiously enough, for I might have waited weeks, I was allowed that information that very morning. A small grey van came rattling down the hill towards me, then suddenly screeched to a halt. Two young men leapt out, ran across the road and made a beeline for one of these bushes. As I passed them they were stuffing one after another of the red berries into their mouths and spitting out the pips. Next time I saw a bush handy to the roadside I followed their example. They were soft, squashy and fleshy, with tiny pips and not much taste while actually being chewed but with a pleasant, elusive after-taste. Not the kind of thing you could eat like cherries: after seven or eight you were tired of them.

The only signs of human habitation there on the open moun-tainside were occasional little stone huts with attached walls forming pens. Wisps of wool clinging here and there gave evi-dence of their function, and sure enough I came across one with its pen full of sheep, their shepherd mending a bit of barbed-wire fence outside and his dog barking furiously at me as I waved at them all and walked past.

When at last I arrived at the Col de Teghime, perspiring heavily but cheerful because it really was a gorgeous morning, I saw there a monolithic memorial and at its base an old German field gun. In 1943 the last fighting to free Corsica from its occupy-ing German soldiers had been just here.

There was a thoroughly satisfying view from the Col of the country between it and the Gulf of Saint-Florent, so I sat down on a rock and prepared to contemplate it for a while. It was a good excuse to cool down. The steep hillside levelled out to a lush green basin, then rose again sharply to a serrated ridge of rocky hills. Between the humps of this I could see the blue Gulf. A couple of villages lay clustered near the foot of the near mountain-side, distant and toy-like. Apart from the bells of a few wandering cows, the shouts of picnicking children and the motor of an occasional car, all was quiet, the sweet silence of high places.

I started to collect my thoughts for the first time since landing, and wondered vaguely if I would be able to complete the round tour of countries on the edges of the Tyrrhenian Sea that I had in mind. Probably not, because it would take more time and money than I had: although time was less important. It was the available money that governed the length of the trip, and already, after starting with less than I had hoped for, I had had to spend far too much in getting here. Three days in Nice. Three days in one of the cheapest hotels in town, which was hardly cheap. Now I could get down to the old routine of buying food in shops, cooking it myself, sleeping in my light-weight single-pole tent at night and tramping along the roads by day. And if the weather stayed like this it could be a promising trip. There was no point in laying any definite plans about getting to a certain place by an appointed time, because of the remarkable uncertainty of the whole expedition. There was always the unexpected.

I ate one of the sweet chestnuts I had found under a tree on the way up and had pocketed, then rose, loaded up and started the downward path. Barbaggio was the first village—I could hear its church-bells already. It was small, compact, pretty, and deserted save for two old men. Patrimonio, further down the winding road, was larger and more scattered. More populous, too: I started offering a 'Bonjour' here and there to test reactions. In some places I've been through, they simply stare at you and stay mute but here, they smiled and said 'Bonjour' back. I passed a lot of tall stone houses, tethered donkeys, cows, pigs and chickens in yards, and some large cavernous sheds with great wooden casks inside, sickly-sweet smelling heaps of purple stuff outside and wasps everywhere, but so far I had not seen a shop. It was still Sunday, but in French territory there is a strong possibility that food shops at any rate will be open. At home, if you are lucky enough to come across a Sunday-opening shop, you can only buy ice-cream and cigarettes and not envelopes and baked beans, which seems incongruous to me. If a shop is going to be open, it might as well sell anything it wants. There was a church in Patrimonio, a big one, old and stylish, in the geometrical Byzantine fashion that apparently prevailed in these parts.

Near the bottom of the village there was a new whitewashed

house that could be taken for a shop. An old woman was shuffling round its side, a grey, amorphous creature with a grey face, grey hair, grey clothes and a grey toothless voice. I asked her if the shop was open, she smiled, and ambled towards its door. This she unlocked and we passed into its interior.

You wouldn't mistake it for a branch of the Home and Colonial, but its shelves, however sparsely equipped, at least offered enough to prevent starvation. I was just making my first purchase and wondering if the old woman was deaf, since she seemed to be having trouble in undertaking what I wanted, when the place was suddenly filled to capacity by the entrance of two men. They were both black-haired, swarthy and youngish, and the older had not apparently shaved that week. They greeted me with flashing white grins, chatted with the old woman in some incomprehensible tongue and appeared to be her sons. They clarified one or two difficulties in my purchasing endeavours and, seeing the light, I asked if Madame was speaking in Corsican.

'Yes, we all speak it.'

'Mother speaks very little French.'

'It sounds like Italian,' I observed.

'Maybe, but it's not Italian, or French. It's a patois.'

'You are not French, monsieur?'

They were delighted, they said, to have an Englishman in their shop. Why I thought, They must have quite a few during the summer? Surely Patrimonio isn't too far off the beaten track? Nevertheless, while the men were engaging me in conservation, their mother disappeared into a back room and returned bearing a bunch of white grapes. 'For you, monsieur,' she mumbled, smiling, 'we grew them ourselves.' She wrapped them up and handed them to me.

'We make our own wine here, monsieur,' the younger man told me, 'the wine of Patrimonio is very well known. Would you not like to buy a bottle?'

I would have liked to, but desisted, for various reasons. It was cheap enough, although an extravagance for a tight-budgeted economiser like me, but the main fact is that a litre of wine is heavy and is too much to be reduced at one sitting by one person, and then it gets too warm when carried in a pack in the hot sun all afternoon. Much later it occurred to me that I might have bought it and split it between the four of us: I am sorry to say that this opportunity for cementing Anglo-Corsican relations was missed. They were so anxious that I should try their Patrimonio wine that the young one went and fetched a small glassful of white wine and dead flies and insisted I should taste it.

'It's very good,' I said, which is what they wanted me to say.

'Our own wine,' reiterated the younger man, 'we made it ourselves.'

'It's excellent. Thank you very much.'

'It is our pleasure, monsieur.'

In the end I compromised by buying a bottle of beer from them. I don't like French beer much but it's the only kind you can get, reasonably enough, in France. It fattened out my modest bill to a figure that made me feel happier about accepting their generous hospitality. I finished the white wine, leaving one or two of the lumpier flies, shook hands all round and prepared to leave.

'We are very happy to have met you, monsieur,' said the older man, his teeth flashing in his black-flecked visage. 'We wish you a most pleasant journey. We are sure you will find Corsica a most beautiful country.'

I ridiculed any possible doubt of this and said *au revoir* about three times. There wasn't much chance of seeing them again but you always say *au revoir* to French people, never *adieu*, just in case. Later on I said *arrivederci* to some Sardinian people instead of the customary *buon giorno* and they thought I was mad. That's Europe for you. Cheerio is at least non-committal.

I did not intend to carry my litre of beer any further than I could help, so when I had rounded a couple of bends and nearly come to the end of the village, just below the fine church, I found a grassy bank under a tree and had lunch. It was good, and the beer, although French and therefore much too gassy, was refreshing—but there were wasps. Still, the sun shone and the afternoon did not involve mountains.

I crossed the green basin I had seen from the Col, between meadows and vineyards, and passed through the ridge of hills. They were hot and desiccated, but on the far side was the Gulf, and projecting into its placid surface was the town of Saint-Florent.

The Citadel of Saint-Florent stands on the highest point of its little peninsula, rearing its old befuddled turrets over the curly-tiled roofs of the town. Saint-Florent is a place of no account now,

although large, as Corsican towns go, but once, in 1794, it was
a port and stronghold important enough to have been defended,
unsuccessfully, by the French against an Anglo-Corsican force
led by the redoubtable Nelson.

Insignificant it may be in the twentieth century, but Saint-
Florent's complacently serene air of having once seen great things,
like a retired cabinet minister, is one of its greatest attractions.
I spent a restful half-hour sitting at a café table in the tree-shaded

Saint-Florent

triangular place bordering the little harbour, watching the Saint-
Florent children playing leap-frog over the rusty old bollards and
the dipping sun weaving silken patterns in pale gold on the
harbour-water.

The sun still had an hour or two left in it, but I felt disinclined
to do more that night than a quick stroll into the hills and camp
near the first available stream. There were sure to be plenty of
streams, there had been on the Col de Teghime road, so I didn't
bother to draw water from a Saint-Florent fountain. That was a
mistake.

I left the town, where they were still enjoying their Sunday-
afternoon game of bowls on the square, crossed the marshes at
the head of the bay and started up the long winding road into the
hills. Not long now, I thought, the first fresh stream will do.

When I had passed three or four dried watercourses I realised how foolish I had been. If there was no water in these hills I could go on all night without finding any. The road was persisting in an upward grind, the sun was sneering into my eyes before dodging behind the dark hills, and I was getting worried. Of course I could camp without water, but I never had: when this sort of thing happened I always had the feeling that if I gave up I should regret it because round the next corner there would be a public fountain or something. However it was a near thing that night.

The road had levelled out to a high plateau, a silent, bare place where there had recently been a very bad fire. Near a blackened stony valley that wound into the hills, I stopped and listened: the musical-box tinkle of a stream. Not much of a one, trickling along the bottom of this valley, but clear and drinkable. There was a fairly level place among the burnt-out gorse bushes on the far side of the stream, so I pitched my tent on this, stowed all my gear inside, then took in as much water as I could from that meagre trickle into my water-bag. This was a creation consisting of a plastic polythene bag with a tap at one end, suspended between two wooden rods. When not in use it could be rolled up and stowed away into the tiny space left in a rucksack for this sort of accessory. This water-bag had already accompanied me on an expedition to Provence, and so far I had managed to prevent it from contact with anything sharp, which hazard was its Achilles heel.

There were mosquitoes in this camp, and also sheep. The chap riding a mule who drove the sheep along the side of the stream while I was frying up by candle-light seemed not to mind me being there: the mosquitoes did. However, the ones I failed to murder during the night were drowned by morning, because there was a heavy mist and I was stuck with my old condensation problem: millions of tiny drops of water all over the tent, inside and out.

It was a fine morning, and if there had not been a hill in the way the sun would have dried me out. It beamed over the top just as I was packing up to go, with the tent still sopping wet. But life is full of vicissitudes and at least the providential stream had guaranteed my morning cup of black coffee, and the countryside, in its subtlest colours, was good. There was a village marked on the map, quite near, called Casta. Much depended on it having a shop, because it was twenty-five miles to Ille Rousse, the next town, and nothing at all in between. I was out of bread and had finished the Patrimonio grapes.

Casta was a widely spread collection of charming old stone houses, looking out from their hillside to the green-stippled rocky ridges and the sea. Its population consisted more of mules and donkeys than people, and it did not rate a shop, or even a bar. I was sunk.

But it was a beautiful day, and certainly the scenery was conducive to forgetting about such little problems. I pushed on cheerfully, admiring the rolling rock-studded hills below and the towering crags above the road. This was the Desert des Agriates, and the term desert was not used in a loose sense: the place was entirely uninhabited and uncultivated. The only signs of life, apart from millions of lizards, were two Bars, some miles apart, both derelict. There were occasional vehicles on the road, of course, but the only other indication that I was not on the moon was a memorial plaque below a roadside cross which told a wretched, tragic tale of some people who had been trapped and burnt to death in a bush-fire some years ago.

By standing on a high point of the road and looking north, I could see vast areas of les Agriates. They reminded me of the high moors in the Scottish Highlands: mile upon mile of stony, rock-strewn hills and vales, with not a tree in sight. The difference was in the basic overall colour. Instead of the sombre brown of heather, bracken and bog there was the lively, patterned green shades of the maquis.

The road, skirting the heights where crows glided over crags eroded into weird surrealistic shapes, climbed up to a pass. Here there was the first level space for miles, a stone shepherds-hut, a terrible heap of old rubbish, and a magnificent panoramic vista away to the South. From the pass there dropped a steep maquis-covered slope to a deep green valley, rising to ridge upon ridge of hills and larger hills and mountains. Over the tops of the dimmest and haziest of these were the vague, cloud-capped outlines of the big ones. They looked far higher than I had expected and I began to feel a twinge of apprehension: my planned route would quite likely take me up one or two.

Having crept up to the pass from the north face of one mountain mass, the road now clung to the south face of the next.

Sauntering down its tortuous contours, whistling a tune, I was surprised to hear a dog's bark coming from up the hill. I looked up
and there stood a man with a shotgun, his dog leaping from rock
to rock barking frantically. Bandits I thought, it's true what they
said about Corsica. Then a bush moved and at once I became conscious that the whole hillside was covered in goats. There were
hundreds of them, long-haired shaggy creatures with horns, in a
wide range of brownish colours. I had not seen them at first because they were the same height as the maquis, which grew tall,
strong and thick all the way down to the uncertain depths of the
valley. I waved to the armed goatherd, who lifted a hand in
response and quietened his dog.

Lunch was a sketchy affair of sweet chestnuts, collected the
previous day, and chocolate. It was not noticeably sustaining, and
it was still a very long way to Ile Rousse.

The first inhabited dwelling since Casta was a farmhouse
perched on the edge of the road above the precipitous bank down
to the valley bottom. Prickly pear grew as a hedge around its yard,
and five dogs came roaring out to see me past. Prickly pear is a
large prolific cactus with a spiky reddish fruit; used as a hedge, it
is better than a barbed-wire chevaux-de-frise, but unless con-
trolled it is inclined to spread and grow everywhere. Further down
there were a couple more houses and another malevolent dog
comprising Monetta. By now I had acquired a monumental thirst
but the faded letters spelling BAR over the door of one of the
houses were sadly false and there was not even a fountain or well
around. Aesthetically speaking, the houses were good, but the
weathered lichen-stained stones, and the warm brown tiles were
rather offset, I thought, by the television aerials.

Then I was back by the sea again; it was azure and serene as
ever, but that didn't help my thirst. Nor, along the narrow wayside of the twisting coast-road which was a kind of shelf in the
steep sea-plunging hills, was there the smallest possibility of a
camp-site. This problem was about to become a regular feature of
travelling in Corsica.

The coastline was beautiful, there was no doubt about that.
The precipitous green-clad hills dipping abruptly into tranquil
water, the clean, white, empty sand-beaches, the irregular fretting
of a hundred bays and promontories and the total absence of
noise: it was superb.

Just as I was grimly contemplating walking the next twelve kilometres into Ile Rousse in total darkness, a car stopped at the roadside ahead of me. Its occupants, a middle-aged couple out for an afternoon ride, offered a lift to Ile Rousse and I accepted with alacrity. Providence again, apparently.

Ile Rousse is another once-fortified, peninsular town of great charm. It has some reddish-coloured rocks, which supplied its name, at the tip of its peninsula, and a lighthouse to mark them. Unfortunately I did not feel inclined to explore it to any extent further than the discovery of a general store and a Bar, because there was not much daylight left. The sun, at that time of year, dipped at five, disappeared at five-thirty, and left no trace by six. This time I watered up before leaving town.

I found what appeared to be a waste plot just out of town on the Calvi Road and pitched camp behind the rusty bones of a derelict lorry. As I was moving my gear into the tent, a young fellow with black curly hair and large moustache came by. Half expecting him to ask me what I was doing there, I was surprised when he said 'Good evening' mildly, and 'won't you be cold to-night?'

'No, I'll be all right, thanks.'

He smiled and nodded. 'Good night, then.'

There was nothing at all wrong with that camp, except for a nearby dog which barked incessantly for four hours.

There was nothing wrong with the morning, either, which fact strengthened my confidence in Corsican weather. I was on the road early and up the hill out of Ile Rousse, revelling in the sunshine and the irregular capes and bays of the northern coastline. The only snag was that this hitherto untamed shore showed a tendency to ominous new building schemes. Huge painted sign-boards announced plots of land being sold off for the erection of summer villas, and presently I came to one that described the new village of Curzo. The village, unlike the summer villas, already existed.

Between the road and the sea was half a mile or so of rough bank, dropping about a hundred feet. A new road led off to it, on the corner of which was a wooden hut, the office and information desk. The village was incomplete and uninhabited as yet, but it was the structure that interested me: none of the regular lines and identical box-houses you expect to find in most new villages.

It was the same old jumble of odd-shaped houses at different angles and levels, steps, arches and all, that you find in any village in these parts which has grown over a few hundred years. This reconstruction of ancient custom was obviously made with an eye to attracting visitors, and bore no relation to the needs of native Corsicans: for that reason the motives of the architects are questionable. Still, there is no denying it makes a pleasant change from the usual run of modern planning.

From the heights just beyond Curzo I could see across a smooth bay to Algajola, which looked like a miniature edition of any of these other north coast fortress towns. A head-of-bay plain lay in between, and behind it a beautiful green maze of wooded hills rising to mountainous heights in the near distance. This, according to a note on my map, was the district known as the Balagne, 'rich in cedars, olives and figs.'

At the foot of the Curzo hill and the beginning of the level stretch, a notice-board at the entrance to a farm track caught my attention. It had been effected by an unskilled sign-writer, and its content, although informative, scarcely even made sense. This translation, however rough, is more coherent than the original:

'1. Balanea. Estate on site of Phoenician town of the god Baal (the eternal lord) called: Balanes by the Greeks, Balania by the Romans (and erroneously, Vapanes), destroyed in the 5th Century, whence it has given its name to this plain and to the province of Balagne and its coins, etc., in the collections: Count Savelli.

'2. San Cipriano, San Cornelio. Roman Chapel (818–XIIIth Century) and its hermitage (1714), on site of one of four temples of Balanea.'

Try as you might, you cannot get the bit about the coins to mean much.

I thought I might take a stroll up the cart-track to investigate, since an additional little sign-board mentioned that all these delights were at 200 metres, but when I had gone about that distance I found the way was blocked by a gate and a No Entry, Private Property notice. I could see the Roman Chapel, a little whitewashed building in a field, but there appeared to be no method of reaching that, either. I began to retrace my steps to the road, muttering about people who put up notices describing antiquities they want kept private.

The site of Balanea, however inaccessible, was not short of

natural beauty. The sea lay in front, the lush arboreal country all around, and the hills behind. On top of one of the hills were what I took for a group of rocks, sharp black outlines against the sky. Pausing on my way back to the Algajola road I turned round and had another look: not rocks, houses. It was a village, perched way up in what must be an incredibly inconvenient position by modern standards, however advantageous it may have been to its builders by way of defence. It was called Sant' Antonino.

Whatever its shortcomings, Count Savelli's notice about Balanea gives some idea of the complex ethnic origin of the native Corsicans. They are nearly as mixed up as we are. Going back as far as we can, to the Neolithic Age, the island was inhabited by Iberian Celts, similar to our early Britons, who erected the menhirs and dolmens still standing in various parts of the mountains (and accessible by complicated and hazardous mule-tracks). Then there were people of a Northern European type, tall, fair, blue-eyed. They must have been extremely clannish because there are still living remnants of them in certain of the more remote mountain valleys. The Phoenicians were only one of the wandering, colonising peoples: in the sixth century B.C. the Phoceans came and founded Aleria, on the East Coast. They were succeeded by the Etruscans and later in the fifth century the Syracusans and Romans. Of course when the Romans started to colonise a place it generally stayed colonised: the conquest of Corsica by Rome took a hundred years, from 260 to 163 B.C., but after that there were no more comings and goings for six hundred years.

Corsica, when eventually subdued, was ruled by a representative of the Emperor and taxed as shamelessly as all the other provinces. Aleria was the principal town—I have not been there but I hear there is little else now except mosquitoes. There was not much advantage in being a Roman province except for the guarantee of protection by military force against all-comers. This was rather offset by the Imperial habit of extracting everything they could get out of the place and putting nothing back in.

As Mr. Gibbon was at great pains to explain, the end of the Roman Empire was not a nine-day wonder, nor a four-hour epic from Hollywood. It was a slow thing, lasting hundreds of years. In the fifth century A.D., about the time when the Britons were rallying under a general called Arturus and fighting for themselves, Corsica was occupied by a tribe of Vandals under Genseric.

They were not particularly aggressive people, once they had found somewhere to live, and did not resist a further colonising attempt, later on, by the Byzantine Empire. Two more centuries, and still the influx of invaders had not stopped. In 725 the Lombards arrived, and a hundred years later the Saracen attacks began.

The Saracens were the least beneficial of all invaders: they terrorised, plundered and burnt, panicked the richer Corsican families into getting away to Rome, and even after two hundred years of occupation left no traces of their civilisation.

The Saracens were beaten in 1034 and finally made to withdraw. They were the last of the waves of settlers, and the modern Corsicans are the end-product of nine hundred years of being vigorously, individually Corsican.

Algajola, on closer inspection, seemed just the kind of place you could stay in for a prolonged session of eating, drinking, and doing nothing. Its very atmosphere encouraged this sort of delicious indolence: no one had even bothered to metal the streets, they were the baked earth and stones they must always have been. The houses stood about at untidy angles as if lacking energy to get in line, the people strolled about unhurriedly, stood on the sea-wall gazing dreamily out to sea or sat for hours gossiping in cafés.

I sat at a table in the café facing the castle and the sea. The castle, an uncompromising four-square mass, was in good condition and inhabited: it occupied the furthest point of the village's little promontory, where the waves splashed against its seaward walls.

I relaxed in my chair under the café's verandah and sipped the red wine; I felt warm and lazy and contented to sit there for ever, watching a little girl play with a cat, listening to the murmur of the other customers chatting with the bar-keeper's wife, and fishing drowning flies out of my wineglass. If you are indolent by nature, as I am, you can very easily be charmed into accepting the leisurely way of life.

But I knew I had to snap out of it; I had to buy stores from a dear old lady in black and I had to push on, up the hill and out of this magic place.

It wasn't far to Calvi and I could have walked there quite comfortably in the day, but when the two-horse Citroen stopped and the two middle-aged ladies in it smiled at me so pleasantly, it seemed churlish to refuse their offer of a lift. I had just passed through the village of Lumio and spotted Calvi, yet another fortified promontory across yet another bay, and there was only the flat dull bit across the head of the bay to do.

Calvi had a bigger and more imposing citadel than any of the other fortress towns I had seen so far. It had its own houses and church and massive ramparts and it stood, on its hump of rock

Lumio

projecting into the bay, aloof from the rest of the town. It was not difficult to see why, for hundreds of years, it had been an important port and naval base.

Two important events, both connected with famous sailors, took place in Calvi. The first, in chronological order, was the birth of Christopher Columbus. By tradition he was reputedly a Genoan, but the Corsican writer Joseph Chiari has shown quite clearly that although legally Genoan, since Corsica at that time belonged to Genoa, Columbus came from Calvi. Colombo, he says, is a name which crops up repeatedly in ancient Calvi records (and still does in modern ones) and there is even the record of a Christopher born to this family at the time when the C. Columbus arrived. So, rage and argue how they will, the Genoans seem to have lost this battle against the Corsicans. Which is fair enough, since for hundreds of years they caused much more than their fair share of trouble and misery in the island: but more about that later.

Nautical event number two in Calvi history was its siege and capture by that phenomenal all-time great of the Royal Navy, Horatio Nelson.

In the year 1794 Corsica, under its aged but still determined leader Pascal Paoli, was rebelling against its French overlords. Paoli, thirty years previously, had been responsible for the finest, albeit pitifully brief, era in all Corsican history (which is another story I will come to later). Having been obliged then to surrender the sovereignty of the island to France, he now took the opportunity of regaining it. The French had magnanimously recalled him from retirement in London to be Lieutenant-General in Corsica, and sent him on a military expedition to Sardinia. This failed, and Paoli was summoned to Paris to explain himself and avoid, if he could, Madame Guillotine. This indignity was too much for the old statesman and he declined to go, appealing instead to Britain to help him reassert his and Corsica's independence.

The Mediterranean Fleet of the Royal Navy in 1794 was under the command of Lord Hood, a gentleman wise enough to listen to the theories and opinions of his most up-and-coming captain, Nelson, who was then thirty-six years old. The French had strong garrisons at Bastia, Saint-Florent and Calvi, so these obviously had to be ousted before Paoli could claim that Corsica was its own master again. Collaborating with Hood, and utilising Nelson's flare for strategy, he was no doubt delighted to find that a force of 1,200 men could land at Bastia and subdue 4,000 Frenchmen. Following this success, in January 1794, expeditions were made to besiege Saint-Florent and Calvi in turn; again Nelson's splendid disregard for convention astonished everyone, including the garrisons of these forts, and with comparatively minute forces, the Anglo-Corsican troops compelled much larger numbers of Frenchmen to surrender.

But it was, as usual, poor Nelson himself who suffered when his genius had won the day for his side: while outside Calvi, directing the siege, a flying splinter of Corsican rock hit him in the eye and blinded him.

Paoli, acknowledging that Corsica on its own could not possibly maintain its independence from France, offered the sovereignty of the island to Great Britain, who, in view of the need for naval bases in the Mediterranean, accepted it. For two years Corsica was British, a period in its history it still recalls, apparently without the least rancour, and which practically everyone in Britain has forgotten all about. It terminated in one of those strategic withdrawals that look rather feeble on paper but probably save a good deal of damage and bloodshed: Sardinia and Italy were conquered by the omnipotent Napoleon, and Corsica, surrounded on all sides by hostile shores, was clearly going to be too hot for comfort. In 1796 the British left Corsica, and the French returned.

After wandering around town for a while, I stocked up with enough provisions to last for three days: according to the map there were no more villages for just the fifty miles from now on. I had a drink at a Bar where a motherly kind of woman anxiously advised me against venturing into the mountains, then I left to look for a camp-site. Half an hour later I returned from the wrong direction, found the right one, and made camp in an excellent terraced field overlooking the bay, with the lighthouse on the Pointe de Revellata winking at me. When the town dogs had silenced, all I could hear was the gentle sloshing of waves on the shore and the high-pitched shrilling of the cicadas (which sound exotic but are really only grasshoppers after all).

Chapter Two

THE WILD WEST

I love to watch little white fishing boats making quiet fish-tail patterns in a blue bay on a sunny morning in late October. It's a comforting sight at any time, but in late October it reminds you that at home the fish-tail patterns vanish in the ruffled wave-tops, the bay would be a gunmetal grey and the whole thing probably invisible because of the fog.

Having crept round the back of the Pointe de Revellata the road from Calvi shook itself free of all houses and went wild. There were any number of little gulfs, re-entrants and ravines for it to negotiate. I could see quite clearly the way it went round the next point but it would take me half an hour to get there, five miles to do two. On my left, the steep green-covered craggy hills; on my right an equally steep drop of a hundred or more feet and then the sea. There were no houses, very few cars on the road, no ships at sea. Once I came across a road-gang taking a rest and a drink by the roadside: it's quite un-usual in Corsica to come across a road-gang actually working. They stared blankly as I approached—they were by a stream at a sharp bend in the road, under the cool trees.

'Where are you going?' they shouted. 'Where have you come from?' 'Are you German?'

'No. English.' Smiles all round, and one little old man, wizened as a gnome, got up and came forward.

'I speak English,' he said, 'where you going?'

'Evisa.'

Horror-struck: 'That's too far!'

'No it isn't. I've got a tent here, I'm camping. What's two or three days? I'm in no hurry.'

What indeed: this was a philosophy they fully understood. The English-speaker grinned and clapped a hand on my shoulder.

'Good for you.' They all shouted and waved as I plodded on up the hill, past their gritty, tar-smelly lorry.

Up to the shoulder of a cape, down to the dizzy ravine of a

stream, the impenetrable wall of hills to one side, the gentle sigh-
ing waves far below on the other: a silent world, where no crowds
blackened and littered the beaches and no motor-fumes fouled the
air.

There were several little streams, and as there seemed to be no
chance of anything stronger that day, I refreshed myself at one or
two. No wonder I thought it was a mirage when I found, on the
col behind the old signal station at Capo al Cavallo, a pretty, inviting little bar. I wasn't missing a chance like that, there might
not be another one for days. A dishevelled, fat old woman, with a
mouthful of black teeth, poured out the wine and hovered, watching me scrutinise my map. 'Going to Porto?'

'I don't know,' I said, 'is it further than Evisa?'

'No.'

'Then I shall go to Porto. Can you get food there?'

'Yes, but it's a long way. There's Galeria, you'll be able to get
bread and things there.'

'Good.' I remembered seeing Galeria, it was just within
reach next day. 'I say, aren't you lonely up here? There isn't
another house for miles.'

'That's true. No one is near, no one.'

But she didn't seem to mind, unduly. There was her husband
there with her, and a big smelly ginger dog. God knows what
trade there was for the bar.

Away from the coast the country flattened out a bit and on top
of an eminence, amid rock-strewn fields and far from any other
habitation, I saw a massive, roofless tower. It was called Tour
Mozza and it had evidently not been occupied for quite a while,
judging from the shattered state of the house and outbuildings,
but it must once have been a place of considerable grandeur. I
felt I should like to have known its history: how such a mighty
mansion came to be built in this wilderness, what happened to
the people who lived there, how long since it was abandoned? It
is of no use asking the local people, they are always the last to give
you any reliable information about things on their doorsteps—
and anyway, what local people? It wouldn't be important enough
for mention in a guide-book, either.

There were a few scattered houses now, about two miles
apart, and one of them was called a Maison Cantonnière, which
I took to mean District House, or HQ for local administration.

There were a couple of bars, one of which was open, some more
break-neck bends and nowhere at all, in view of the westering sun,
to pitch a tent. I climbed up to the col on the Pointe de Ciuttone
and sure enough there was a flat grassy space where the road
levelled out briefly before plunging downhill again, I had just got
set up there and was thinking about dinner when there came an
almighty crash from outside and then voices raised in acrimony.
Two cars, one approaching the col from each side, and driving in
the normal Corsican fashion in the middle of the road, had come
to a logical conclusion. The debate sounded exactly the same as a
drivers' dispute in any language: most of it was bad. I suppose
they must have come to some arrangement because eventually
they dispersed; when I went out at about nine in the evening, all
was quiet. I could see the lights of Galeria across the gulf, and
over on the other side a car light moved along the black cliff-side.
I couldn't hear it, and it would be a good ten minutes or more before it reached my col, the road twisted so much. A fine night,
with just the waves and the cicadas again.

A goatherd, arriving by car at the col, woke me at seven in the
morning. He let the goats out of a pen somewhere further down
the hill and they tinkled all over the maquis-covered hump between the col and the sea.

I made an early start and trotted at a fair pace down the winding road to the Gulf of Galeria, which was really the estuary of the
Fango river. Galeria village, the first since Calvi, was not on the
road: to reach it you had to follow a lane along the far side of the
bay. I rested for a while, sitting on a rock at the wayside, considering whether or not it would be worthwhile to do the four
kilometres to Galeria and back to lay in more provisions. It would
take two hours to get back to this spot, and then I'd not be able to
cover anything like the number of miles through this unpopulous
wilderness as I should.

I compromised by buying apples at the lonely Hotel Fango,
at the riverside, then set off up a long, deep valley, inland from
but parallel with, the coast. The road twisted, uphill all the way,
for seven miles, closely following the hill contours; no one lived in
the valley, the only house, apart from a few shepherd huts, was
the Maison Cantonnière de Colomba, and that was empty. Like
the sea-coast hills, these were violently steep; tributary streams
crashed through jagged chasms in their sides and hurtled down to

the bottom. Up them, away from the road and in the bewildering jungle of the Forêt de Tetti, was the most savagely rugged country I had ever set eyes on, steeper, even wilder and lonelier than those mountain glens in the Highlands. There were not many cars along the road: at times I had the whole dramatic valley to myself.

About half an hour after lunch I reached the Col de Palmarella. From it I could look back along the length of the valley, right down to the Fango. Black, ominous clouds were beginning to gather over the far peaks: the fine spell about to break up, perhaps? Look the other way, out to sea: all blue sky, sun, serenity. My next objective was the Col de la Croix, which I could easily see, only about three miles away, between the main landmass and the two-headed Mont Senino, separating the Golfe de Girolata and the far-away Golfe de Porto. By now I was getting used to the way Corsican roads behaved and was not surprised to find that the three miles would involve five more and take two hours. There was a massive re-entrant where a stream coursed down into the Golfe de Girolata, and several tributary ravines, and the road had to creep round the edge of the lot.

It was eerily silent. No one was about, the only signs of life apart from crows, pigeons and thousands of little lizards, being a few straying cattle, sheep and goats, all belled. Like a lost world: if war had been declared, you'd never know about it here. Once I thought I heard a faint, distant rumbling, and still full of the if-war-broke-out fancy, imagined at first it was bombs, or guns. But it was probably thunder in the mountains, which was still, although somewhat diminished, an uneasy notion.

A rare car was standing near an excellent fountain which gushed from a pipe into a stone basin and subsequently down into the valley: its occupants, a middle-aged couple, were finishing a picnic. They greeted me politely and watched as I unrolled my plastic water-bag and held it under the flow. It was getting on for four o'clock and there might not be another source of water: I was beginning to learn about travelling in this country. It was a bit of a nuisance having to carry the water-bag, and I was now on the long stretch of road that crept along the side of the main mass, which meant that the setting sun was in my eyes. Still, it was not far to the Col de la Croix now, and there would probably be a place there to camp, there usually was at the cols. There was certainly nothing along here even remotely possible.

I passed a car that was parked at the roadside. A young couple near it transferred their gaze from the scenery, which was worth looking at, to me, who was not. We exchanged waves and I plodded on up to the Col, which was only a kilometre away now. Suddenly the car was at my elbow, and the young man, a good-looking lad with dark curly hair and fine features, was leaning out of his window asking me if I wanted a lift. I was not at all sure at that moment if I did, because it was not far to the Col and I was sure to be able to camp there, but nevertheless I accepted. The driver's companion was a pretty dark girl with an attractively soft voice; she asked me the usual questions about myself and I explained that all I wanted was a little bit of field in which to put my tent. I must have been more tired than I had thought, because I should have known that field was a word almost unknown in Corsica, in this part of it at any rate, because there aren't any. They misunderstood me.

We roared over the Col, where there was a place where I could have camped, and started zig-zagging down the other side of the mountain. We passed a little village under the south shoulder of Mont Senino, called Osani. We thrashed wildly round the hairpin corners and pretty soon I was feeling very hot and rather sick. 'We can take you to Partinello,' said the youth, but no further because we are taking some people from there to Porto. You will be able to find a place in Partinello.'

In Partinello? Funny . . . but I was not inclined to enquire further: if only he wouldn't drive quite so fast round these corners. I sweated away in the back seat and we rattled through a village called Curzo. We had been able to see Partinello for some time, splashed up a hillside, but of course there were seven more downs, fourteen ups and fifty bends before we got there. It was five o'clock and the sun was setting. We pulled up outside an inn, and I realised that they must have thought I had said *chambre* instead of *champ*. I apologised and explained, and they understood and grinned and waved goodbye and there I was standing in the streets of Partinello with about half an hour's twilight to play with and the whole performance of finding a camp site and erecting my tent to fit into it. Several villagers were hanging around, sitting on the roadside stone wall and chatting. One old man called out to me.

'Where are you going?'

'I'm looking for somewhere to camp.'

He treated this as quite normal, although in this perpendicular place and at this time of year it must have been a sign of madness. 'Ah, well now, you saw the fountain when you came into the village? Well, there's a little path down from there, that's the place for you. No, it's not private property.'

His companions laughed. Nothing appeared to be private property hereabouts. I thanked him and went back through the village to the fountain, past several suspicious and malignant dogs. I remembered the fountain and had no difficulty in finding it, but the little path was more of a problem because it didn't seem to exist. I could see what he was getting at, there were a few terraces carved out of the hillside with vegetables and fruit trees growing on them, but there was nothing but a locked gate and a suicidal drop by way of access to them. The place really was ridiculously steep.

What then? I searched along the road frantically for a few hundred yards, then a few more, turned a corner out of sight of Partinello and in sight of Curzo. Nothing: not one space the size of a postage stamp that wasn't either solid rock or angled at forty-five degrees. By now the sun was down and in ten minutes it would be dark.

Employing a vituperative turn of phrase to express my opinion of the situation, I hurried back to the village for a last desperate search for the little path down from the fountain. And found it: a little steep pathway further up from where I had looked before. There was a gate but it was not locked, and there was a fine, secluded piece of grassed terrace just wide enough to accommodate my tent.

It was pitch dark when I had finished erecting it and supper was by candle-light. I was exhausted, having come a long way and been on my feet all day, but before crawling into my sleeping bag I went out to look at the night. And in it I saw and heard two things I had never seen or heard before, even though I could easily have done in my own back garden at home: I saw a glow-worm and heard the ghastly cry of a screech-owl.

A long, strenuous day deserves, in my book of rules, a short easy one to follow. The thunder in the mountains had not materialised in Partinello anyway and it was another clear sunny morning, except that my terrace was in a position where the sun hardly

ever shines, so the tent was wringing wet inside and out with
mist, dew and every other kind of moisture but rain. Partinello,
a pretty village on an unbelievably violent slope, although possessing a church, three bars and several new houses in building
(which I took to be a good sign) did not apparently run to a shop
—or a postbox—but I admit I didn't venture further up it than I
had to, so it might have, all the time. I left the village and sauntered lazily along the avenue of eucalyptus trees to a col overlooking the Golfe de Porto. The road thereupon did its customary
detour all round the hills, the river beds and the cliff-edges and
ended up at sea level, where a turning in the upward direction led
to Serriera. Since this was advertised as one kilometre away, I
thought I would take a look at it and see if it was more forthcoming in the way of shops and postboxes than Partinello. I was
glad I had.

Serriera turned out to be a delightful little place, tucked away
in a fold of the hills, and although technically a dead-end, far
more colourful than that epithet implies. People, mostly women,
stood about in the street gossiping: I asked one group if there
was a shop in the village and got a most courteous and friendly
response. The man in the shop was fat, unshaven and morose,
but he had all I wanted. Every time I asked him for something
he would shout 'Maria!' and bawl out a string of Corsican. In
would come Maria, as thin as he was fat, and find it for him.

On my way back down to the main road an elderly man on a
donkey stopped to pass the time of day with me. He too was
warmly interested in my doings, cheerful and glad that I was
enthusiastic about his Corsican scenery. At the end of the Serriera
turning, were more donkeys,the place was full of them.

There was now a steep sweaty climb up to the next col; near
the Serriera end it passed a bar where half a dozen workmen were
sitting at tables on the verandah reading newspapers and arguing.

From the col I looked down over the Golfe and saw the little
village at the mouth of the Porto river and a ruined watch-tower
on a heap of rock. Porto village, standing further up-country from
the estuary, was full of houses built in the local salmon-pink
stone, quite a number of which were brand new. Feeling like a
drink, I stopped at a bar, and who should come out to serve me
but the lad who had given me the lift to Partinello, last night. It
was only when he asked me if I had found a satisfactory camp-

site that I recognised him, because the only part of him I remembered clearly had been the back of his neck.

It was at this bar, while the lad was being chased by another and laughed at by his father, mother and little sister, all of which noisy and hilarious activity took place outside in the street, that I had my first Casanis.

Pastis, or anisette, is one of the most popular drinks in France. One calls to mind Pernod, Ricard and Berger; they pour out a dram of yellowy-gold liquid, you add water and it turns to cloudy yellow-grey and tastes like peppermint. It is cool and refreshing, and if you go in for it wholeheartedly, cheering too. In Corsica they do not have a surplus of wine: most of what they make is exported. Accordingly the Corsican taste has decreed that pastis shall be the national Corsican drink, and out of all brands of pastis, a Corsica/Marseille product called Casanis. In Corsica it was at that time (and probably still is) from eightpence to tenpence a glass. At home a Pernod costs three and six, but then the beer situation is so much better. From Porto on, I became a Casanis addict.

A little lane led up the north side of the Porto River Valley to a village called Ota and the mountain mass where, at 2,700 feet up, there stood Evisa. The lane was steep and mostly tree-lined, and on my perspiring way up, I met a donkey. It seemed a sociable creature, so I made friends with it, but I didn't expect it would follow me for the next mile or so. I was thinking I had solved the pack-carrying problem for the rest of the trip, but then we came to a chestnut-tree. I stopped to pick up a few nuts, and offered one to the moke. He crunched the lot, spiky shell-case and all. I gave him a few more, and he got the flavour. I filled a pocket with nuts and went on, he stayed behind, eating. So much for that wild hope: I would have to go on being my own donkey after all.

Before reaching Ota I noticed several little chapels, mostly in the classical style, shelved into the slope above the road. These all had a name over the door and several wreaths lying about and were in fact family mausoleums. This practice seemed to be quite common in Corsica: in some places, notably Sartène and Olmeto, the houses of the dead were so numerous they constituted a town almost as big as that of the living, a whole hillside-full of domes, columns, porticos and the symbolical cypress trees.

When I approached Ota, I thought the whole population had turned out to meet me, because the street was full of sombrely dressed men and women, gathered together and chatting quietly. The church bells were ringing, dirge-like, and presently the priest, in full vestments, arrived with two censer-swinging acolytes. There was no real need to ask what was going on, but in case it was the Corsican way of celebrating the outbreak of war or something similar I asked one of the men present. The answer was what I had expected—a funeral. I found a bar, a drink and a chair, outside on a little roadside terrace, and started a sketch, because the way the village was perched precariously on its hillside, with dangerous slopes up and down and great frowning mountains curtaining the valley like theatrical backdrops, was eminently sketchworthy. Presently the funeral procession got under way and came slowly past, and I stood up for it.

First came a choirboy bearing the big gilt cross, then the women, all in black. One of them, practically the oldest by her silver hair and pale, deep-lined face, carried a silken banner showing the Virgin and Child. Then came the priest and a stately old man, chanting alternate lines of the funeral dirge, and finally all the men and the hearse, a black van. The men were visibly less grief-stricken than the women, I even caught two or three of them chatting and grinning among themselves. All the time, the church bells droned on in a solemn rhythmic pattern. The procession crept slowly up through the village. I could imagine it coming to rest at one of the little mausoleums, the doors unlocked, the priest chanting long Latin prayers, the air full of incense, the black-shrouded women weeping, the men all now serious: the ritual of death playing its important, significant part in the lives of these Corsican mountain people.

I was excited by the way the tall stone houses of the village reared up so high on their impossible platforms and terraces, by the way little flights of steps wound up to them, by the colourful splashes of purple bougainvillea spilling over walls and climbing balconies and verandahs; and by the dramatic beauty of Ota's situation.

Having by now, some idea of the difficulties of finding suitable camping places in this sort of country I went into the bar and asked its occupants if they could recommend one near the village.

'Yes,' said a hoarse, hairy old reprobate playing cards with a crony, 'at the end of the village, either to left or right, anywhere there.' This time I didn't stop to enquire if it was private property or not, I just hoped he realised I wanted something a bit more level than the usual forty-five degrees. I watered up at the village pump and followed the directions out past the last house. There were terraces, difficult of access but excellent in quality. I chose one, three tiers above the road, and lay listening to clanking cowbells and the roaring Porto river way down in the depths.

OTA,
PORTO VALLEY.

There was rain in the early morning, the first of the trip, but it stopped by seven. On my way down to the bridge over the river, I met one of the old women in black who, I think, had been in yesterday's funeral procession: she too was white-faced and silver-haired. We passed the time of day, and she said, 'Why not take the footpath if you're going to Evisa? It only takes two hours that way.'

This sounded reasonable, especially as it would probably take four by the road, so I asked where it started.

'By the two bridges. It's only a mountain path, you understand, but very beautiful.'

'I'll try it.'

'You will want to see La Spelunca, anyway, won't you?'

Doubtless, but I had no idea what La Spelunca was. It was marked on the map and underlined in blue, but it was no more explicit about its nature. I thanked the old woman, who had just been watering the flowers round her family's mausoleum, and went on down the road. It was intensely complicated, but it seems it was necessary first to go two kilometres up the valley to cross the river, then two kilometres back again on the other side to join the other road from Porto and proceed on the tortuous mountain route to Evisa. As I mentioned, the whole thing would involve immense effort and at least four hours. If the footpath was practicable it would be both rewarding pictorially and time-saving— not to mention energy-saving.

The bridge, or bridges, were at the point where the Porto river was joined by another, coming in from a gorge to the north. The path began on the south side of the Porto bridge: a notice-board confirmed the old lady's assertion that it was but a two-hour trip to Evisa. I paused on the bridge, as a few other early visitors were doing mostly with a view to fishing, and admired the scenery. It was impressive, almost bewildering: the mountains towered up, sheer on all sides, the rivers rushed and gurgled, met under the bridges and foamed and roared off down the valley to the sea. Being at river level meant that in order to go anywhere, you had to do a lot of climbing.

I started off down the path, with misgivings. I remembered a similiar occasion when I was looking for the Chartreuse de la Verne, in Provence: the path had led me gaily on for a while, then petered out. This one started off in fine form, with a surface rather worse than the path up Ben Nevis, but plain to see and liberally strewn with donkey droppings to show the way. But after half a mile my forebodings were justified: the path split and stopped by the riverside. There was no way across the river and there was no way round the cliff that cut off further progress. Exasperated, I trudged back to the two bridges: I would just have to tramp it out up the road, after all.

It was a long tramp too, and irritating to be going back the way I had come, if on the other side of the valley. I saw Ota again, all of it, and then rounded the corner to join the Evisa road out of Porto. It doubled back towards the head of the valley again, towards those bridges, but on a much higher level.

Although there wasn't much level about it, just an endless upward slope, but the scenery, from those heights, gained in majesty. There was Ota again, a midget village of toy houses and a little toy church, miles away down there on the far side of the valley, a splash of white, grey and black on the green curtain. It was impossible now to see the river, and nearly impossible even to hear it. Ahead the mountain tops loomed nearer.

From the Col de Capicciolo I saw the most astonishing piece of topography, I think, that I have ever seen. I was high up a mountain, and in the mountain there was a great, deep, sheer-sided cauldron. At the bottom of it, a stream hurtled down to join the Porto, which was roaring out of a towering, massive gorge, a canyon. Great bare rock-faces frowned their scarred, fissured countenances all around, so nearly vertical that it was difficult to see the tormented waters at their bases. I am not good at heights, and to go near the crumbling edge of the road, and look down into those awful, unimaginable depths cost me a feeling of nausea. One wouldn't call it beautiful, it was stark, diabolical grandeur, like a thunderstorm. This was what the Corsicans call La Spelunca.

Apprehensively keeping to the inner edge of the road, I skirted this nightmare, and from one point could see where, at the very bottom, the path ran by the side of the Porto. I had gone wrong quite early on, the path kept to the higher ground where I had gone down to the riverside, but there was no earthly means of getting down to it now. Higher still, the road climbed away out of the cauldron and gave on to another, much milder version, green and pastoral and full of chestnut trees. Far away, up in the mountains, I believe I caught a glimpse of the houses of Evisa. For some completely unknown reason, clinging to the sides of this chestnut-lined basin, two villages had been built. They were both higher than the road I was on, both tiny, but both fully inhabited: at Chidazzo a whitewashed church peered above the trees, at Marignano thin grey smoke rose from the tall stone houses. This was the most fantastic country. Now I was obliged to follow the road all the way down to the river again, cross it, and sweat all the way up the other side, in the same double-back fashion as before. When you travel this road, you get to know the river Porto and its valley pretty well! Further up, at some points, I could catch a glimpse of the sea, hard by the peaks of Les

Calanche, the mountain mass bordering the southern shores of the Golfe de Porto, and at others, yet another view of Ota. Near Evisa the chestnuts thickened and the country, at a height of rising 2,400 feet, began to look like an English park.

This high, gentle-sloping grassy parkland is known as la Chataigneraie, the Chestnut Country. The chestnut trees are huge, and their nuts are the biggest I have ever seen. Occasional pigs rooted in among them, and sometimes a group of women would be gathering nuts and loading sacks of them on to donkeys, but far more than would be collected seemed to be left lying, to rot. Something ought to be done about that, I thought. This really was the most fantastic country. First the deep green Porto valley, then that frightful sheer-sided chasmal cauldron, seemingly bottomless, then this charming oasis, high among the mountain-tops.

Near the beginning of Evisa I saw where the footpath emerged. Heaven knows in what fashion it climbed up those dizzy heights, it must have been almost perpendicular, and I felt rather glad I had lost it.

Most of Evisa is on either side of a long uphill main street. A lot of it was big villa-type houses and hotels for summer visitors, which at this time of year were closed and shuttered up. The centre of the place was where the real Evisa people lived, and was therefore livelier. I did some shopping, then found a bar, where there was a little boy continually running in and out, the first newspaper I had seen in three days, and a plump, pleasant-faced woman. I was heartened to find that she was not shocked or surprised by the lateness in season of my perambulation, so it couldn't really be so cold up there in the mountains.

I did a couple of kilometres out of Evisa, through the rest of the chestnut country, and entered the Forest of Aïtone, in the valley of the river of that name. The terrain had gone slightly vertical again by this time and the only place I could find for camping was in a pine wood, sloping sharply down to the river. The weather, sultry all day, had now clouded over and darkness came quickly. I had only done about fourteen miles that day, but most of them had been uphill. The funny thing was that, as the crow flies it was only about five to Ota from Evisa. Not that a Corsican crow would know much about that, the ones I had seen were just flying round in lazy circles, like everybody else.

Chapter Three

THE MOUNTAINS

Owing to the fact that this pinewood camp was on a rather drastic slope I could only sleep on one side. In the middle of the night I had to get up, reverse myself and the bed in order to sleep on the other side. In the morning it was perishingly cold (I had slept in all my clothes anyway) and I was nearly through the lower end of the tent. The wood was on the north-facing slope of the Aïtone valley, which meant that it hardly ever got any sun, and certainly not in the morning. I hurried everything along, packed up and left half an hour earlier than usual, and hurried off up the road to the Col de Vergio at a furious pace, to try to warm up.

It was a beautiful morning; it may have been the fresh mountain air, or the sight of sunshine dappling the road through russet and yellow leaves, or the springy carpet of pine needles at the edge of the road, a joy to walk on, but I felt exhilarated and full of exuberance. 'On top of the world' is a ridiculously trite phrase, but this is what it felt like. Possibly being on top of about four thousand feet of it helped.

The Col de Vergio, which I reached after this intoxicating canter of five miles (all uphill), is actually 4,830 feet above sea-level, higher than the summit of Ben Nevis. It is a neck, as its name implies, between two much higher mountain masses, and connects the Aïtone valley and forest with that of Valdo-Niello. I sat down on a rock on the Col, ate a couple of chestnuts and contemplated the huge basin in the mountains that lay before me. It was thickly wooded on the south side, open, stony and sunlit on its northern slopes. It stretched for miles and miles, fading indistinctly into more grey-blue shapes in the far distance.

There was a chill wind up there on the Col, so I did not stay long. I was off down the long road, through the pines and lovely silver birches and their kaleidoscopic pattern of dark green and yellow against the vivid blue of the sky. Save for a few isolated forestry establishments, there were no houses, this side of the Col

39

or the other. The road dipped and twisted gently through the forest, over hundreds of little sparkling tributary streams burbling down to augment the Golo river, which was the basic reason for the Valley of Valdo-Niello.

It was curious, but although this whole day's journey was much higher than yesterday's on the road overlooking the Porto River and La Spelunca, there was hardly any illusion of height at all. Even from the Col de Vergio it was no more vertiginous than standing on the North Downs at Wrotham or Detling and looking out over Kent. So there was no justification at all for my early amendment of the name to Col de Vertigo. For one thing the slopes here were gentler, the valley bottom was not so far down, there were no dank black rock faces, and most of the time you could see nothing but trees anyway.

There were cars about, because it was Sunday and this was the kind of place people drove out to see, and while I was lunching by a fountain so that I could wash down my meal with fresh clear water, one pulled up alongside. It was a large flashy car, a Mercedes-Benz, and out of it merged two large men, both bearded, and a little boy. While the boy was filling bottles at the fountain, one of the men, dressed in knickerbockers, saw me and came up for a chat. He was curious about my presence there, so I told him the reason—that I was walking around in Corsica because I wanted to write about it.

'Ah,' said he, 'you should go and see ledderose in Ajaccio.'

I obviously didn't understand and he repeated it a couple of times.

'What,' I asked, 'is this ledderose?'

'It is a lady, Ledderose.'

'Oh, Lady Rose!'

'But of course! She is English, but she has lived in Corsica for twenty years and knows all about it, history and people and everything.'

The other man from the car mentioned that she was the Corsica correspondent of the *Daily Mail*. Knickerbockers, in a rather self-important way, insisted on giving me her full name and a vague address, as well as his own.

'When you are in Ajaccio,' he said, 'go and visit her. She will tell you all about Corsica.'

They climbed back into their big car and left. I sat there,

finishing my meal and picturing myself, dressed like a tramp and probably by that time smelling like one, making a social call on Lady Rose!

At lunch I was eleven kilometres from a place called Albertacce, the first village along the valley. I had already done pretty well, having started so early, so I promised myself a drink there and camp outside it. It was still beatifically sunny and when I had shaken free of the tall pines I felt the benefit of it. I could now see the Golo gurgling along a wide bed in the valley bottom, the scant pastures and stone walls on the northern side, and several huge peaks rearing into the tranquil sky, of five or six thousand feet or more. Monte Cinto was one of them, the highest in the island: it is around 8,900. These were the awe-inspiring monsters whose uncertain shapes I had seen from that pass in the Desert des Agriates.

I crossed the Golo and came into some more chestnut woods before Albertacce. There were people among them collecting the nuts and sacking them, as they had been at Evisa. In Albertacce, a pretty village set in a fold of the valley's hills, I had a couple of Casanis outside a bar, warm in the afternoon sunshine, and chatted with a couple of young fellows. Both, in answer to my polite query, proudly claimed to be Corsican and of Albertacce itself. I made some flattering remarks about the Valdo-Niello scenery, and asked them about the chestnuts.

'Do the people harvest the chestnuts for sale in the shops? They fetch good prices in the towns.'

'That is so, but most of them collect the nuts just to feed to the pigs, and for Christmas. You know,' he grinned, 'after the chicken and sausages and ham, come the chestnuts.'

Both these young fellows were well-built, tanned and healthy-looking, with the usual Corsican black curly hair and open, pleasing features. One of them, in an ex-army camouflaged jacket, was asking me if I had met any bandits.

'Aren't you afraid of walking in the mountains alone? What about the bandits?'

'Oh, bandits,' I laughed, 'I don't believe there are any. They died out years ago, didn't they?'

They admitted it was true: a pity, because a bandit or two would help add a touch of spice for the tourists, but there it was. No more bandits.

While we were chatting lazily and sipping our drinks, a large black dog came sauntering up, and I absent-mindedly scratched its head and ears. At once it apparently conceived a consuming passion for me: when I stood up and prepared to go, it stood up. When I loped off down the road with my bag-full of water from the fountain, it followed. It watched me climb a terraced hillside, select a site (like a billiard-table compared with last night's pine-wood) and make camp. Then it stretched out beside the tent and prepared to spend the night there. I didn't mind in the least, until it saw fit to guard me from all-comers. That meant barking non-stop for half an hour. I shouted at it and swore at it and threw things at it, and eventually it was quiet.

It still growled occasionally, while I had my supper, watching the sun setting behind the hills in lovely bands of orange and pink and listening to the Albertacce church bells playing an attractive little tune to the quiet valley. When I crawled out later in the evening to sniff the air, the black dog was still there.

It had gone by the morning, which was rather cold but not so exhilarating as yesterday. I sauntered past a sequestered small convent into Calacuccia. This was a larger version of Albertacce, on the same south-facing slope but near the end of the Valdo-Niello basin. It had several shops and bars, a big new Post Office and a resplendent hotel, but apparently only one bakery, and that was closed. I was not likely to run into any more shopping centres that day, so it was a good thing I had bought a packet of veritables in Albertacce. Perhaps I ought to explain that in France you can get a kind of toasted rusk which are rather brittle but keep well, if you don't mind eating the last three in forty-five little pieces; these are called biscottes, and the most popular brand bear the tag, 'les véritables biscottes'. You acquire some funny habits when travelling alone, such as referring to kilometres as killies, and general stores, called alimentations générales, as aliment shops, and Albertacce as Albert. It all sounds slightly mad, but as there is no one else to hear you, it doesn't matter much.

Calacuccia, with or without bakeries, was an attractive place in delightful surroundings, and to reach it, if you come from the direction of Corte and Bastia, you have to pass through an astonishing piece of scenery called La Scala di Santa Regina. The lad in the camouflage jacket outside the bar in Albert—sorry,

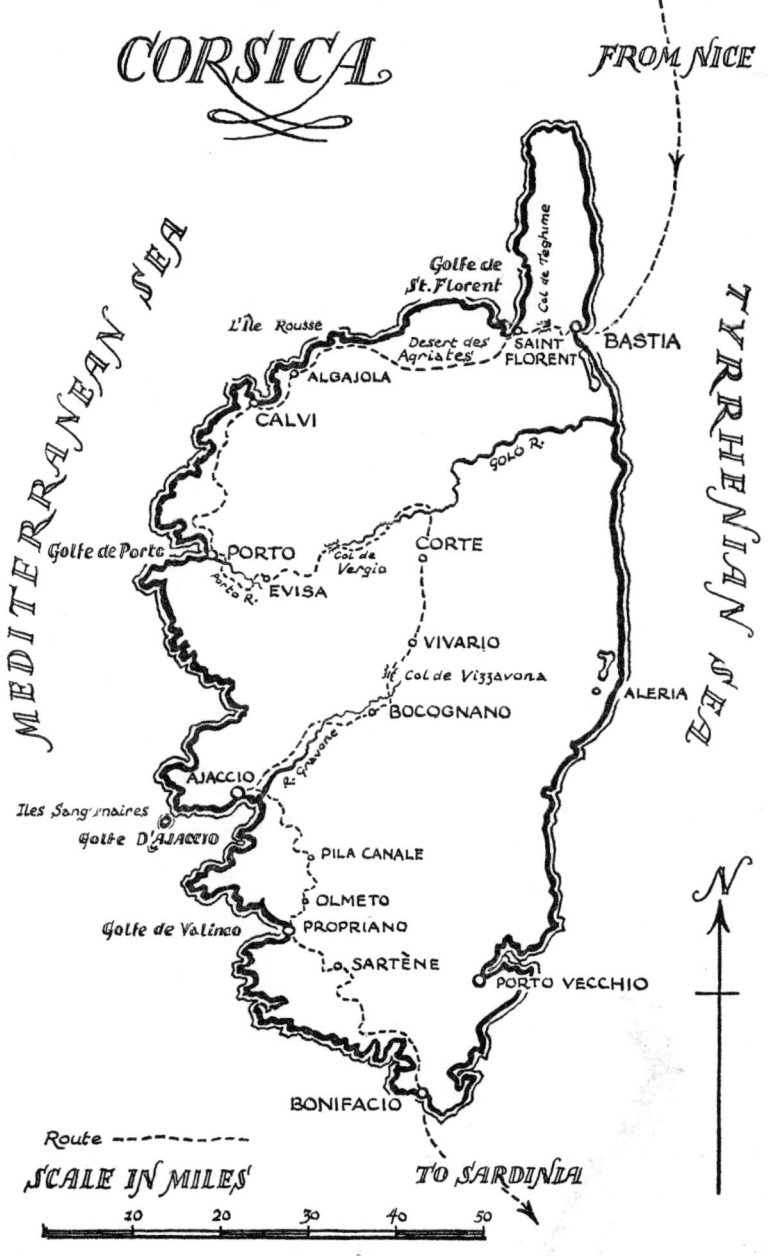

CORSICA

FROM NICE

MEDITERRANEAN SEA

TYRRHENIAN SEA

Golfe de
St. Florent

Col de Teghime

L'Île Rousse

Desert des
Agriates

SAINT
FLORENT

BASTIA

ALGAJOLA

CALVI

Golo R.

Golfe de Porto

PORTO

Col de
Vergio

CORTE

Aitto R.

EVISA

VIVARIO

Col de Vizzavona

ALERIA

BOCOGNANO

R. Gravone

AJACCIO

Iles Sanguinaires

Golfe D'AJACCIO

PILA CANALE

OLMETO

Golfe de Valinco

PROPRIANO

SARTÈNE

PORTO VECCHIO

N

BONIFACIO

Route ----------

SCALE IN MILES

TO SARDINIA

10   20   30   40   50

Albertacce—had told me that, if I was going that way, I must on no account miss La Scala di Santa Regina.

'What is it,' I asked, 'a church?'

He looked puzzled. 'No, it's a place.' But I still had no idea what sort of place until I came to it and saw for myself.

At this lower end of the Forest of Valdo-Niello, where the Golo River, gathering strength and volume from the myriad mountain springs, thunders and gurgles and crashes from side to side in its wide, shallow bed, there are several little villages, strung out across the valley and the hillsides on the end of narrow white lanes like a chair-o-plane roundabout at a fairground, with Cala-cuccia as the central pivot. The last of these is Cuccia, nothing more than a hamlet of half a dozen houses. It lies at the foot of a solid wall of rock that hems in the end of the valley: millions of years ago it must have presented the Golo River with a challenge, because the result is an exposition of the old 'irresistible force meets immovable object' hypothesis. The Golo, exerting the kind of force that has made hydro-electricity possible, has smashed its way into the solid thickness of the mountain and scoured out a gorge, many hundreds of feet deep and seven miles long. Sheer bare rock, eroded into weird, fantastic shapes, looms up almost vertically on either side; the road clings desperately to the northern side and follows the vicissitudes of the jutting mountain buttresses, the whole length of the way. Like La Spelunca, no one could call La Scala di Santa Regina pretty, or even beauti-ful: it is majestic, cataclysmic, apocalyptic if you like. I am glad I walked along it, because traversing it by car would be like crossing the Atlantic in a submarine.

There is only one inhabited house along the length of La Scala, a small-holding with pigs, cows and desperately terraced postage-stamp strips of thin soil. Also four dogs, which may be a comfort to the smallholder, but bellowed at me for half a mile either side of the place.

Just at the point where the shadows of nightmare begin to crowd in and you think you are doomed forever to crawl beetle-like along the bottom of this awful chasm, you turn a corner and the whole character of the place changes. There are milder, greener slopes on either side with trees, the maquis, and a couple of roadside buildings on a bend that look exactly like bars, which by some miracle they are.

La Scala
de Santa Regina

RuL

Two men were strolling up the road towards me, from the nearest bar. Perceiving that unimaginable object, a person walking the
roads as if he enjoyed it, they stopped and greeted me. One was
middle-aged, rotund, swarthy, and like the Reverend Chadband,

had a general appearance of having a good deal of train-oil in his system. It presently transpired that he was a Spaniard. His companion was much younger, a good-looking young Corsican with black hair, blue eyes and a perennial sun-tan. We discoursed for a while on the subject of my travels—the Spaniard's French was terribly accented. I mentioned that I had in mind an extension of my tour of Corsica to Sardinia and North Africa.

'Tunis?' said the young Corsican. 'I wouldn't go there, if I were you, not on foot with a tent. It's full of Arabs, a terrible thieving, murdering lot. Much too dangerous.'

'Rubbish,' said the Spaniard, 'they're not like that at all. I've been in Morocco, and Tangier and Algiers, and met hundreds of them. They're all right.'

'Anyway,' I put in, to mollify the Corsican, 'there are plenty of French people in Tunis too.'

We discussed the beauties of Corsica—geographical, not feminine, I had yet to see any outstanding examples of the latter —and I mentioned a few of the places I had seen and admired.

'Yes,' said the Corsican, 'ours is a beautiful country, all right. The trouble is, there's so little work.'

'That follows,' I agreed, 'because most of the country I've seen is impossible to cultivate, and there's nothing much apart from agriculture. No mines, or industries like that.'

'No, that is true,' he sighed, 'that's why so many of us have to emigrate, in order to live. It is tragic, because all Corsicans are passionately fond of their homeland, but it cannot support us.'

They started to move off up the road towards their parked car. 'One day,' the Spaniard smiled, oozing a little, 'you must travel like this through Spain. It would be worth your while.'

I promised that one day perhaps I would—and I might— and waved them round the corner and out of sight.

The second of the two bars looked the more pleasant, so I went in for a couple of cool Casanis. They were served by a Madame Mutton dressed hideously as Mademoiselle Lamb. Her atrociously dyed yellow hair and stage make-up reminded me of something I saw once in Berwick Street, or it may have been Frith Street. It was not pleasant. *Sans faire rien*, however, because the pastis was just as good and as inexpensive as anywhere else.

Ponte Castirla is a hamlet at the junction of roads at the very end of the Golo gorge, where a bridge crosses the river for the first time since Valdo-Niello. There was no bakery there either, so I gave up and lunched on veritables, then pressed on up the valley of a Golo tributary. From Castirla, a village built quite inconveniently on what really amounts to a cliff-face, was a fine view over the lower Golo valley and a jumbled heap of hills fading away to the coastal plain, which I could not see. The Golo emerges from the hills and ejects its waters into the sea close to the southern end of Bastia airport; in fact Ponte Castirla is only about thirty-eight miles from Bastia, so I had almost come the full circle.

However, I was now heading south to Corte. Trudging up the side of a tributary valley, most of which appeared to have been recently burnt, I couldn't help pondering on what the young Corsican had said about there being too little work in the island. There was a good deal of land here that might be difficult to cultivate, but surely not impossible? It was not devoid of vegetation: what about all these wild olive trees, and cork-oaks, and eucalyptus? Acres and acres of wild scrubland in these valleys, just waiting for someone enterprising enough to take them over.

I sweated up to the Col d'Ominanda, crawled over it, and stood looking at the town of Corte, spread on and about a sudden crag in a small basin in the mountains. It was about four kilometres away and I had no intention of going there that night. I thought of doing about half of it, to show willing, but the coincidence of a fresh stream and a good grassy terrace just over the shoulder of the Col was too much. After dark, the lights of Corte made a splendid, romantic sight, and the sound of falling chestnuts, whipped off by a fresh breeze that had come skipping over the hilltops, failed to keep me awake.

The breeze matured into a cold, definitely unpleasant wind, which persisted in coming up in great violent gusts, like a mistral, all the next day. I trotted down the four kilometres into Corte and arrived within its precincts by ten o'clock. It was important that I should get there reasonably early, because I was down to my last franc and needed urgently to cash a traveller's cheque. Corte was a decent-sized town, something on the lines of an English provincial town, so I was sure it would have plenty of banks. I was wrong.

Travellers' cheques are a remarkably ingenious invention. They save carrying around large amounts of notes and coin and the constant worry of having the said currency stolen. They are, however, about as much good as a used bus ticket when there's nowhere to change them.

I walked the length of the Cours Paoli, the main street, looking for banks. Not one! I stopped a pair of strolling policemen, one of whom was short and fat and the other tall and thin—they could easily have just walked offstage after an encore of 'The Bold Gendarmes'—and asked them for banks.

'Yes,' smiled the short, fat one, clearly delighted to think that someone expected him to know the answer to anything, 'there is a bank. But it's closed today.'

'It'll be open again on Friday, though,' added the tall, thin one very helpfully.

I got them to direct me to the Post Office. I didn't think the Post Office would cash travellers' cheques, but you never know.

I *should* have known: they would not. 'Why,' said the bored young man behind the counter, 'do you not try the bank?'

'Because I have just asked a policeman, and he said it was closed.'

'No, no, that's not right. It opens Tuesdays and Fridays. To-day's Tuesday, so it is open.'

'Oh, that's all right then.' I knew those policemen weren't real. 'Where is it?'

'In the Cours Paoli, next to the Café Cyrnos.'

That was right enough, and there was a notice on the door that said open Tuesdays and Fridays, but it was, nevertheless, closed. I asked a man in the Café Cyrnos if it was likely to open in the afternoon. He didn't know. Then I went into the Air France office further along, and asked the woman there if she would change a traveller's cheque. She would not, but she was as con-cerned as I was about the bank being closed, because she wanted to use it.

'If I were you,' she suggested, kindly, 'I should wait until two o'clock, when it is due to open after lunch. I'm sure it will, be-cause I haven't heard anything about it not opening all day.'

It was then eleven in the morning, so I had three hours to kill. That was not difficult, because Corte is a fine old town and there was plenty to see, but it did mean that I could not go into any of its museums, because I hadn't the entrance money, and there was a very strong, cold wind blowing. I couldn't even go and sit at a café table and write postcards, because I couldn't afford the postcards and I couldn't afford a drink, but the three hours passed. Later on, I will mention what I saw in them, but first I must finish this story.

At two o'clock I went and stood outside the bank. The bank, incidentally, looked more like a betting shop than any bank I had ever seen, which somehow made it seem even less likely to function as a bank. It still looked dead, but I was presently joined by a sergeant in the Foreign Legion, and this cheered me up somewhat. The Foreign Legion had a barracks just outside the town, half the traffic in the Cours Paoli consisted of legionnaire-filled trucks and jeeps. The Foreign Legion don't wear blue coats and red trousers any more, they wear khaki, but they still have the white kepi—it's a kind of symbol.

The banker, said the sergeant, was supposed to come in a car from Bastia. Plenty of cars came, and some parked quite near, but none of their occupants turned out to be a banker. At about two-thirty, a drinker at the Café Cyrnos informed us that the banker would never come today. There was a fête, he said in Bastia, and his presence was needed. The drinker seemed a reasonable kind of character, a young man of an intelligent cast of countenance, so I explained to him my impecunious predicament and the frenzied need for money.

'Mmm,' he said, scratching his head, 'you could, perhaps . . .'

'Yes?'

'. . . try the chap in the S.N.C.F. office. He might help, he's a good sort.'

I waited in the Railway office for a good five minutes before anyone came into it. He was younger than I expected, a heavily built fellow in his thirties in a neat dark suit and a neat dark hairstyle to go with it. I went through my explanatory spiel again.

'Let me see these cheques,' he said. Clutching hope, I flourished the plastic wallet, full of the things.

'No,' he sighed, 'I'm sorry, I cannot change these. You'll have to go to Bastia, or Ajaccio.'

'How?' I asked, calmly. 'I have exactly one franc, fifty-five centimes. That is not even going to get me to the station.'

'Oh! I can see you have a problem. One moment: perhaps the man in the bar next door will cash one of these cheques. Come with me.'

But the man in the bar next door gave me a nasty look. I might have been an Italian, or an Arab, or some other kind of criminal foreigner. No, he would not change one of those improbable scraps of green paper into good French francs. Did I take him for a fool?

Back in the S.N.C.F. office I tried a last desperate tactic. I had in the back of my wallet four slightly shop-soiled English pound notes. I extracted two. Could monsieur perhaps change these? That amount of money would at least take me to Ajaccio.

Monsieur examined the condition of his own wallet. It was a little delicate that day it appeared, but could still summon enough energy to change places with one of the pound notes. Thirteen and a half francs of it did, forthwith. Just then he glanced up and spotted a friend passing in the street. He leapt out and dragged him into the office, petitioning for the exchange of the other pound. The friend, quite unperturbed, said little. He merely pulled out a gigantic wad of notes from a pocket and peeled off two or three. I found myself holding fourteen francs. 'The rate's thirteen fifty,' I said, 'and I haven't got the other fifty centimes change. Could you . . .'

'Oh, don't bother,' said this Rockerfeller, smiling faintly, 'it's all the same to me.'

So I had twenty-seven francs, fifty centimes, and it would just have to last until I reached Ajaccio. The whole point of this story is, that Corte is the third largest town in Corsica, of a size that in most countries would rate three or four full-time banks, yet it has only one miserable sub-branch. By a quirk of fate I had arrived on one of the two days it should have opened, and by a further quirk it didn't. If you're touring Corsica, be warned and carry cash.

Corte is built on and around a sort of excresence of rock that rises out of a small plain, surrounded on all sides by the mountains. It is thirteen hundred feet above sea level. The nub of the place is the Cours Paoli, which starts at the north end of the town, runs straight across the foot of the rock and ends in a square called Place Paoli. On top of the rock is a castle which was built in 1419 by Vincentello d'Istria, one of a long series of Corsican heroes in their interminable struggle against the colonising Genoese. It is not a particularly exciting castle, but its site on the pinnacle of that surprising crag is romance in itself. The crumbling, tottering

houses lining steep cobbled streets all the way down to the Cours
Paoli are more than enough to get any artist, photographer or
romanticist into a state of frenzy. Half-way down there is a
square, in the centre of which is a statue of Jean-Pierre Gaffori.

PALAIS NATIONAL
FROM PLACE GAFFORI,
CORTE

RH

The square is named after him; from it there is a flight of old
worn steps leading through an ancient archway to a large, austere
building called the National Palace. In itself this is not remarkable, but it has become a sort of national shrine, because it recalls the palmy days of Corsica's short-lived independence, for
which they fought so long and so persistently.

The Genoese, despite the exertions of heroic native leaders like Vicentello d'Istria and Sampiero Corso, in dominating the island for so long had exploited it as cruelly as the Romans before them. After a hundred and fifty years of frustrated impotence since the last (Sampiero's) rebellion, the Corsicans in the 1720's were ripe for another one. The spark was kindled in 1729 by one Lanfranchi, of the village of Bozio, who refused to pay his taxes. The rebellion was raised, the rebels occupied Bastia and demanded terms. A short truce having been broken, they occupied the whole of the northern part of the island. The Genoese, whose power by this time was declining, were obliged to buy the military assistance of German mercenaries, eight thousand of them with thirty cannon, under the Prince of Wurtemberg. It took the rebels some weeks and a few minor defeats to assess the real worth of the Germans, but when they did they beat them so soundly that the gallant Prince, in May, 1732, signed the Treaty of Corte and left with the remains of his army.

But Genoa was not content to leave it at that: as soon as the Germans had gone they took a different course. By blockading the island's ports they reckoned on starving out the rebels. In vain, the Corsicans asked Spain for help. Then someone in England heard about it, and the traditional English sympathy for any gallant minority fighting against an oppressive majority resulted in English ships breaking the blockade and revictualling the island.

Then there came a curious and rather comical interlude, when in March, 1736, an adventuring opportunist called Theodore von Neuhof landed in Corsica and volunteered to be King. Like all confidence tricksters he was a smooth-talking villain and the Corsicans, in dire need of a leader, elected him. It was not long before they discovered that von Neuhof's words spoke louder than his actions. Like a pre-election politician, he made plenty of promises, but when it came to the push there was never a remote chance of him keeping them. By November of the same year the Corsicans had got wise to him and indicated that the privilege of having him as King was a luxury they could do without. He left, and incidentally came to a sordid end in the debtors' prison in London.

Genoa, in its final stages of decadence, now called on the French to subdue the rebels. And in two years eight thousand

Frenchmen succeeded where eight thousand Germans had failed. When they departed the leaderless Corsicans were beaten, and the island became a bone of contention in a dog-fight between the French, Genoese, English and Germans. While they were at it, however, the Corsicans were finding the leaders they needed. Jean-Pierre Gaffori stirred them up again, united them and inspired them to breathe fire at the Genoese. By 1753 he had become enough of a nuisance to rate a special Genoese assassination, but this time the Corsicans had an even better chief to succeed him. This was a young man named Pascal Paoli.

Paoli, while the Genoese were too feeble to do anything more constructive than a judicial assassination, grabbed the initiative. Although politically still under Genoese sovereignty, he set up an all-Corsican, native-born democratic regime and governed the country from his capital, Corte, as if it really was independent. It worked so well, with the enthusiastic co-operation of every Corsican man, woman and child, that European eyes began to turn on the island in wonder, admiration and envy. Praise poured in from all sides, and after the moral encouragement, something a bit more practical by way of commercial aid. In June, 1765, Paoli founded the University of Corte, and it seemed, with Genoa incapable of doing anything about it but look on and gnash its teeth, that nothing could go wrong now. It could, of course, and promptly did.

In 1768, as a last-ditch economic measure, Genoa sold to France the sovereignty of Corsica. Paoli, full of confidence, sent a delegation to Paris to put in what he must have felt to be the formality of a plea for the continuation of his independence. It failed: France wanted Corsica for her own. Paoli appealed to all those erstwhile admirers of his regime, all those 'friends' of his little democracy. Like Prince Charles Edward Stuart's English Jacobite supporters, when it came to it their sympathy did not extend to doing anything concrete to help. It meant fighting: it meant that the tiny army of Corsicans had to slog it out against the crushing power of Imperial France. Curious how the fate of the Corsicans' fellow Celts, the Highland Scots, runs parallel: denied support by alleged allies, they took the field in a last desperate stand against an overpowering enemy and were crushed. As at Culloden, 1746, so at Ponte Nuovo, 1769: the fight of the Celt for his ancient, independent civilisation and his defeat and destruction by one more modern, more robust and more brutally vigorous. At Ponte Nuovo the slaughter was unparalleled even in Corsican history.

By one of those odd but somehow inevitable chances in history, on the very day that France declared Corsica a part of her territory, the 15th of August, 1769, Napoleon Buonaparte was born in Ajaccio. It seems a pity, for the sake of justice, that we cannot record the full extent of this irony, that Napoleon would eventually raise Corsica to the heights again; but he never had time to

CORTE

worry much about Corsica and after a brief visit in 1799 never even saw it again.

Paoli escaped the disaster of Ponte Nuovo and managed to get away to refuge among sympathisers in England, where he stayed until recalled twenty years later to be a Lieutenant-General in the French Army, as I have said when I was talking about Anglo-Corsican activities in Calvi.

The same worrying gusts of wind blew me out of Corte that had blown me into it. It was eighty-three kilometres, mostly uphill, to Ajaccio, but as it was also three o'clock in the afternoon I didn't feel like doing more than about three of them before camptime. On the way out I passed by the colossal barracks of the First Regiment, Foreign Legion. The guard on the gate was dressed up in his lily-white kepi, fancy red epaulettes, B.D. jacket,

a sort of beige cummerbund with a black belt, knife-edged creases
in his trousers and boots with a shine fit to shave in. I have seen
in my travels a great number of French soldiers, but I have never
seen one with anything like the dash, personal pride or, to use a
French expression more often employed by the British Army,
esprit de corps, than this legionnaire. It must be about the only
regiment in the French Army with a tradition strong enough to
withstand modern amalgamations and inconsistencies. I walked
past this representative of a legend, wondering for a moment
what would happen if I went and volunteered. Instant certifi-
cation of lunacy, I should think.

I cut the kilometres to Ajaccio down to eighty, found some
water, and camped in a pleasant grassy meadow below the road.
It was a good camp, with a fine open view across a wide
valley to the mountains on the far side, and it even had mushrooms, which went down well with the evening fry-up. It was
also, which was most important, sheltered from the wind.

I don't often see the dawn, because I hardly ever get up early
enough. In point of fact I didn't really get up to see this one: I
woke early, realised that if there was a good one I was facing the
right way to see it, unzipped the tent flap and watched it from the
comfort of my bed. This particular dawn was like a Brahms sym-
phony: a splendid beginning, a gradual development, working
up to a pitch of glorious anticipation, and then just when you
expected the thunderous chords of some great climactic theme, up
came the grey clouds to cover it, subdue it, to trail away into
obscurity again.

The clouds soon dispersed and it was a grand morning, calm
and sunny. I carried on along this pleasant wide valley until I
came to a place of several villages. One of these was Casanova:
there had been in Corte, near the Post Office, a statue of one,
Comte de Casanova, but I don't know if he had any connection
with his amorous namesake. When you think of it, Newton or
Newcastle is a pretty common name for man and place in
England, too. I left the main road and went up to Saint-Pierre de
Venaco, which was grouped on the top of a hill, a quiet huddle of
flower-grown old stone houses. I went into the village shop, where
the young storekeeper was talking with a splendid old character in
Corsican corduroy, his jacket slung cloak-like across his shoulders,
his white beard, moustaches and eyebrows jutting fiercely out

from beneath a wide-brimmed, low-crowned hat. I imagine he was a patriarch of the village.

The storekeeper, a dark-haired, fresh-complexioned man in his early thirties, was extremely helpful in showing me all the varieties he had of the kind of food I usually bought, and we began chatting. He was from the village, had lived there all his life, and appeared quite content to continue to do so for the rest of it. I told him where I had been, and his eyes shone with proprietorial pride when I extolled Corsica's beauties.

'In my opinion,' he told me, 'you have already seen the best part of Corsica, in the north and west coast. It is the most wild, the most unspoilt. In your tour you will have seen most of the finest country in the island.'

To save me going all the way back to the main road, he very obligingly took me by the arm and indicated an alternative back way to Venaco, the larger village of which Saint-Pierre was a limb. It was a lovely, quiet, meandering way, in and around the green tree-covered slopes, and I came to Venaco, quite a large place, strung out across the hillside with wonderful outlooks across the luxuriant valley, in a remarkably cheerful frame of mind. This was dampened slightly when I chose the wrong bar for a drink: it was run by a surly old misery who had managed to impose his cumulo-nimbus personality on the atmosphere of the place. I kept, with the other customers, a frigid silence, and was glad to finish my drink, pay up and creep out, back into the sunshine.

Now came the gruelling drag up to Vivario. The scenery was typically Corsican and therefore gorgeous: a narrow, deep green V-shaped valley, a river tumbling along its bottom and the road winding relentlessly along its serrated side. What distinguished this, the Vecchio valley, from the others was the railway.

Part of the romance of railways is the engineering challenge to run them through the most difficult country imaginable. There are some pretty remarkable railways in Switzerland, but this one, from Corte to Ajaccio, almost equals them. It is only a single-track line, but it involves countless bridges, tunnels and viaducts, it performs unbelievable contortions to gain and lose height, and achieves a climax of burrowing under the 3,831-foot Col de Vizzavona. At Vivario it doubles back on itself in a hairpin movement, to gain a thousand feet. It was quite a long time before I saw or heard a train on it, but they turned out to be fast little single-car affairs, well adapted for the tortuous task of negotiating all the bends and wriggles and gradients.

Pont de Vecchio, two-thirds up this first valley, was where the Vecchio emerged from a deep gorge in the mountains. Its chasm was crossed by two bridges, one high up for the railway (and if I was the engine-driver I'd shut my eyes at that point) and the other, directly beneath it, for the road. Nearby I noticed two memorial crosses, where a boy of nineteen in 1953 and a girl of eighteen in 1954 were killed in road accidents. I have a note, which I made that night in camp: it says, 'It must be the way these lunatics drive.' Any kind of careless mistakes or excess of speed on these awful roads amounts to suicide—or manslaughter for the passenger: yet I hardly saw a car that was not screeching hectically round the bends and roaring up and down the hills. Familiarity breeds contempt, and contempt of these Corsican roads is lethal.

Vivario, from its considerable height, surveyed the whole of the Vecchio basin down to Venaco. Although the main link road between Corte and Ajaccio ran through it, the traffic was not heavy and it managed to preserve its air of bucolic leisure. Quite a number of its inhabitants were standing about in the streets, chatting, men rode slowly about on donkeys and mules, women loitered at pumps and fountains, gossiping while they filled glass flagons: Vivario ignored the petrol tankers that toiled noisily up its zig-zag streets, it had its dignity to think of.

Within a quarter of an hour of passing Vivario's church, I was looking down on it from a great height, so rapidly does the road scale the mountainside. However, by the time I had crept up to the crossroads where the road from Ghisoni and the celebrated Col de Sorba joined mine, there wasn't much rapidity about my movement. Among the mountains again, and still climbing, I was now in the thickly wooded Forest of Vizzavona. The sun had for some while now been obscured by a bank of dark cloud, and the dense pinewoods crowded gloomily in from all sides. I trudged through Tattone, an insignificant hamlet distinguished by a fine new sanatorium; the road wound relentlessly up, ever steeper, ever gloomier. The village of Vizzavona lay somewhere off the road in the valley bottom, but apart from a few roofs it might not have been there at all for all I could see of it. It was not far now to the Col de Vizzavona, but I had had enough.

Opposite a forestry house was a track leading down into the woods and a sign, 'Camping des Américains'. I had no doubt that the place would be closed for the winter, but just to make sure I went up to a shed where a couple of young men were fiddling with part of a motor belonging to a yellow tractor, and asked them where it was. One mumbled something and the other ignored me, so I shrugged and went on down the path, and quite soon found my own place, without troubling les Américains. It was about 3,300 feet up, cloudy, and threatening rain: evidently another occasion for sleeping fully dressed.

The rain began at about a quarter to four. It eased off now and then, but it is very difficult to sleep with it beating away at the length of thin canvas an inch or two over your head. The intervals were not long: it never took me long to effect my ablutions but I had to run back, half-way through them. I waited until half past nine, then struck camp at the speed of light and made a dash for it. Before I had even reached the road it was bucketing down again. I struggled the two kilometres up to the Col, sheltering now and then under trees, but still it rained. There were houses on the Col, summer residences now all closed and dead—there was also a kind of clammy mist. It presently occurred to me that I was walking through a cloud.

On the highest point of the Col there were the black, shattered fragments of a castle, an awful dank, slimy place. Its position was probably of great military importance, but it must have been hell for the garrison. At last I was pounding down a wet, slippery road, dodging the oil tankers grinding up through innumerable gears round the breakneck corners, down out of the clouds. The rain eased off, and I could see ahead again, and what I could see made me stop and stare.

I wish I were a landscape painter, for the dramatic grandeur of that picture could be better expressed on canvas than in words. On either side, the sharp, ragged diagonals of black mountain plunged down to a woolly cushion of dull green vegetation: in its midst the gleam of water from the Gravone river, whose whole long course opened to view, a mild, hazy jumble of hills and trees and water fading to the grey shapes of the far hills. Overhead, great lowering masses of grey and blue-black cloud surged majestically across the turbulent sky, while below, like the apocalyptic outriders, ragged wisps of grey stormed over the mountian spurs and dashed against the uncompromising harsh rock-faces. *Götterdämmerung:* the Twilight of the Gods, a natural saga demanding thunderous chords of Wagnerian intensity. A distant bar of pale blue sliced across the horizon, promising relief from the turmoil of the mountains.

I could just see the roofs of Bocognano from that head-of-the-valley vantage point, about five miles away. It took most of the morning and two more rain-showers to get there, but with the first houses of Bocognano looming up at last the sun broke through, flashing brilliantly on the wet road. I might have known it would make it once I broke away from those dismal mountains. There was quite a lot of Bocognano before it amounted to anything; I passed its church, looking damp and neglected (although no doubt it was not) and noticed its belfry or campanile, in the usual Corsican style, tall, slender, square, minaretted and detached from the church, standing on its own.

I called at the first general store I came to, and was greeted affably by the pale, wispy young lady serving and by a large, swarthy, balding individual with horn-rimmed spectacles, who was her father and the proprietor. At this juncture I needed to restock with such basic essentials as sugar, coffee and cooking fat. I didn't think there was any hope of getting cooking fat, so I asked for oil, but it only came in huge bottles. When I explained about the cooking fat, to my great surprise, they produced some, a sort of dry compound of vegetable fat. This was the cue for conversation. We established that I was English, not German, and I found myself answering a sort of questionnaire in order to justify my apparent departure from my senses in wandering around the Corsican mountains, on foot, out of season and consequently in filthy weather. It was difficult. Eventually I said I was a sort of writer, and from the fuss they made you'd think I had said I was Somerset Maugham. To change the subject I came out with my usual conciliatory, but perfectly genuine, line about the wild loveliness of the Corsican hinterland. Again, as in the eye of the young Corsican I met in the Golo gorge, there came that sad, troubled expression to the proprietor.

'Yes, but we are a poor country. There are only three or four million of us in Corsica, and still there is not enough work to go round. We have no factories, you see, nothing for the young men to do for a permanent living, and not enough agriculture to support them.'

After a great deal more inconsequential chatter, in the course of which Monsieur informed me that as he had a schoolmaster cousin who lived in London, he would certainly write to him so that I could go and visit him when I returned home, he insisted on giving me a bottle of Patrimonio wine, a rosé. I was, I hope, suitably grateful for this, and left with their valedictions ringing in my ears, but in the confusion of trying to pack all the rather bulky things I had bought, into my rucksack, I forgot to pick up the change from the ten-franc note with which I had paid for them, and so inadvertently paid for the gift. Carrying the bottle of wine, I then had a chase round Bocognano's back streets, enquiring here and there, after a bakery. Eventually I tracked it down to the back door, quite unheralded, of the house of another of these dear old white-haired ladies in black. All the people I solicited for directions were instantly friendly and helpful, in fact I only had to ask one person and at once three or four more clustered round to put in their bit. It was a heartening experience.

Most of my lunches, although tasty and sustaining, were not exciting. This next one, which I had early because I was hideously overloaded, was wonderful. I will describe it, because although it was about the only lunch I had that was worth describing, it just shows what can be done if you put your mind to it and meet a generously-inclined shopkeeper.

First there was bread and paté; the paté was of hare, recommended by the young storekeeper of Saint-Pierre de Venaco. Then there was bread and a biting, vigorous cheese called Bluet that I had bought in Corte: this was the main course. It was followed by fruit (a banana) and chocolate, and the whole feast was encouraged by the Patrimonio vin rosé. You may think that drinking wine out of a yellow plastic mug perpetrates unspeakable atrocities to its flavour. Let me tell you that it does no such thing. Who—having at his disposal a bottle of wine and a yellow plastic mug as his only receptacle—would sully his delectation by cavilling at details?

Lighter in load and head, I tottered on down the smiling green valley. Down from the mountains now, no more rain. Just a long straight road, by the Gravone's banks, Ajaccio, then the warm south.

But the clouds were massing again, even down here in the Elysian Gravone valley, and mountains or no mountains it was obviously quite soon going to rain like hell. I scooped some water from a stream which was breaking its neck to rush down and join the Gravone, and made rapid camp in an adjacent gravel-pit. I was just in time: with myself and all my gear inside the tent, down came the rain. Defiantly I cooked a good dinner and washed it down with the rest of the wine, and soon the rain left off. I felt I had won some kind of victory.

How wrong I was. The only times, that awful night, when it wasn't battering rain against my long-suffering canvas, some wretched, officious dog had to come and bark at me, incessantly. Sleep? You're joking.

Chapter Four

AJACCIO

It was a non-committal sort of day, overcast and humid; the tent was saturated and therefore heavy, I was in urgent need of sleep and not at my brightest, and the most exciting event of the morning was seeing a train on the railway. The Gravone valley was pleasant, wide and verdant, but still remarkably uncultivated. There were a few minor factories, mostly for making concrete blocks and a gradual intensification of traffic towards Ajaccio. Several lorry-drivers and motorists stopped and offered me a lift, but I turned them all down because I thought it would be best to get into Ajaccio early the next morning, which was a Saturday, visit the bank and then have the rest of the day to inspect the town and get a decent distance from it before nightfall. As it turned out it would have been more sensible to accept the first lift going, but that's life for you, full of little surprises.

At a place not even marked on my map I called at an inviting bar for a couple of vivifying Casanis. Madame la Patronne was a generously constructed lady of a voluble disposition. She proudly exhibited to all her customers her gigantic baby, which was like a bull-calf. Most of the conversation was in Corsican, and therefore unintelligible to me. I found that nearly everyone used it, and yet I never saw it written down, on signs or posters or even house names. Other minority langauges, like Gaelic in Scotland, and Basque, and Provençal, have become commercial properties, their 'cuteness' flamboyantly splashed about to attract the tourists. You find huge notices outside Highland towns simpering 'Ceud Mile Failte'; hotels in the Basque Country called Euzkadi or Etcheverria; and ghastly table-mats on sale in Saint-Tropez inscribed 'Lou gai solei me fai canto'. And yet, proportionally, far more Corsicans speak their own language every day than any of the others do. Perhaps, with the advent of the Tourist, Bringer of Wealth, to Corsica, their ancient tongue too will be exploited—and killed at the same time. What use is Corsican when the tourists can only understand French?

Slipping in a word edgeways when the other customers had left, I asked the buxom Patronne if she knew whether or not the Ajaccio banks opened on Saturday mornings.

'I don't think so . . . I don't know. Wait a minute, here's my husband, he'll know.'

Her husband could have passed for an Italian film star: the silvery wavy hair, the aquiline profile, the air of having once been a great lover, the charm of manner.

'The banks? In Ajaccio? Oh, I think they do. I'm sure they do. Wait, here is Pierre, he will know.'

This was a friend, so insignificant beside this glorious Adonaic being that I cannot remember a single thing about him.

'Yes,' he stated with immense conviction, 'they do, but only until twelve o'clock. They are closed in the afternoon.'

Well, that was all right, then, and the uneasy feeling I had, that I had been foolish to refuse all those offers of lifts, was quite extraneous.

The day brightened towards its end: from some places along the road I could see the Gulf of Ajaccio shining like grey silk, shot with pale yellow sunlight. I reached a main road village called Mezzavia, some four or five kilometres from Ajaccio, at about three in the afternoon, and decided to stop there. I had a leisurely drink in a small bar, watered up, and extensively explored a strip of rough common land opposite a large football stadium before settling on a place to camp. Even then it was not very level, but the sky was clear and stayed that way, and I could almost hear the cicadas above the roar of traffic.

Ajaccio, seen from half-way across the Gulf, looked large, expensive and attractive, a splash of white buildings in a deep green setting, between azure water and lapis lazuli sky. The general effect was rather spoilt, I thought, by huge rectangular modern blocks of flats rearing up over everything, but even they were subdued by the noble hills behind the town. The outskirts were as dreary as the outskirts of any large town, but the Cours Napoleon, running parallel with the dockside, where the Compagnie Générale Transatlantique's ship *Napoleon* was moored, started the long trek into the town centre. There were more bars than shops along this undeviating street, but I wanted neither. I found the banks, all in a small area of side-streets near the Post Office.

They were all closed.

They didn't open on Saturdays at all—ever. I laid a soul-scorching curse on the head of the wretched Pierre, whose face I could not remember, and went dejectedly to the Post Office to ask if there was any alternative source of exchange. Waiting in line for my turn at the Post Office counter (the Post Office was an imposing building in the classical style with steps like Saint Paul's), I had a ghastly 'déjà-vue' feeling of Corte all over again.

The counter clerk recommended a travel agency in the Place Maréchal Foch. I went there, and suddenly felt wholly conscious, for the first time, of my steaming shabby tramp-clothes. There was a gorgeous red-head, all haute couture and an intoxicating mist of perfume, and she had to tell me twice that she couldn't cash my travellers' cheques before I could concentrate.

'Oh dear,' I said, hardly believing she could be anything but generous. 'Er—do you know anywhere else I could change one?'

'But yes,' she smiled, and made my day. 'There is a shop, in the Cours Grandval. It sells pieces of Corsican Art, for tourists.'

She was right, bless her, and at last I was in possession of an adequate supply of francs (minus a pretty steep commission, of course). I celebrated in an adjacent bar, at an outside table in the sunshine, where the Cours Grandval faces the Place de Gaulle, the Casino and the sparkling sea. Lovely to relax, soak up the warmth of the sun, sip an iced pastis, and watch the people of Ajaccio sauntering unhurriedly about in the square: no worries, no problems.

A little while later I was sitting on a bench at the end of the Place Foch, having lunch. The Place Foch is aligned, more or less, with the Cours Grandval, but whereas the latter runs parallel with the waterside, the Place Foch is at right angles to it. This is because the two thoroughfares are on either side of the promontory containing most of old Ajaccio, including its citadel (still occupied by the army). One of the most important houses, by a historical circumstance, in the old town, is the one in which Napoleon was born.

The road that runs along the dockside waterfront of Ajaccio, to my left as I sat looking out over the Gulf, is called Boulevard Sampiero. I doubt if there is a single Napoleon story which has not been told and retold many times, but until I started reading about Corsica I for one had never heard of Sampiero Corso.

Which is remarkable, because his story is as epic a drama as ever was invented for mere entertainment.

Sampiero Corso was born, in 1498, in the village of Bastelica, which is a few miles south of Bocognano. He was brought up in a tradition of hatred for the Genoese, who by their intolerable oppressions and iniquitous extortions had been abominated and resisted by the Corsicans for generations. At the age of twenty he left home and began a military career by joining the guerilla forces of Jean di Medici, from which he graduated to fight for the French in their endless succession of minor wars. He was a good soldier and in the course of the years he rose from the ranks to a position of eminence, which was enhanced by a flamboyant offer of sacrifice to the French king. It was in Rome, in 1536, when this opportunity arose to cover himself in glory. France was at that time at war with the Emperor Charles V of Austria, and had been since 1520. By attacking and annexing large portions of Northern Italy, France had become a serious menace to the Austrian Emperor. At first the French had lost heavily and been driven out of Italy and across the Alps, and the Imperial troops had invaded Provence. But after a courageous decision by the Provençaux to defend only Marseille and Arles and dismantle all other fortifications, leaving the invading army at the mercy of organised Provençal guerillas, the Emperor, failing to subdue Marseille, was forced to withdraw. His army's retreat through the ravaged Provençal countryside was a disaster, to the effect of leaving twenty thousand corpses along the road to the Alps.

Charles V was back in Rome by 1536. Sampiero Corso proposed to King Francis I of France that he should assassinate the Emperor, and then jump in the Tiber: by drowning himself, he would have killed two birds (the Emperor, and the blame for his assassination) with one stone. King Francis refused the offer but recognised Sampiero's loyalty and valour: he put him in charge of the Corsican infantry brigade in the French Army.

The peace of Crespy, in 1544, finished the long war at last: no one gained anything by it, and I have no doubt there is a moral in that somewhere. Sampiero returned home to Corsica and in 1547 married a beautiful lady of noble family considerably younger than himself. But this was no marriage of convenience; Vannina d'Ornano loved her husband with an intensity that compelled her to accompany him on fresh campaigns around Corsica against the Genoese. For year after year she shared his troubles and discomforts and privations, soothed his ills and injuries, and rejoiced in his victories.

Genoa was allied to the Emperor Charles V, which fact induced the French to come to the aid of the Corsicans. A French expedition landed at Bastia, and the Corsicans, under Sampiero, joined it. By 1556 Genoa was defeated; the Corsican Assembly asked King Henry II of France to accept responsibility for their island, and he agreed. For two years Corsica was free from Genoese, and Sampiero and Vannina were able to relax in comfort. But they should have remembered the old injunction about putting your trust in princes. At the Treaty of Catcau-Cambresis, in 1558, King Henry handed Corsica back to Genoa and poor Sampiero was back exactly where he had started. At sixty years of age it was apparently the cruellest stroke of fate possible, but despair then led to black, wretched tragedy later.

He escaped from Corsica with his wife and small son to France. Vannina and the boy stayed in Provence, while Sampiero, accompanied by his secretary, Antonio Saint-Florentino, toured the courts of Europe asking for money and support for his renewed campaign against the Genoese. The crafty Genoese waited until he was far away in Constantinople, then sent a message to Vannina indicating that if she were to go to Genoa with her son, she might be able to procure a pardon for Sampiero. Fortunately Sampiero's spies were as efficient as the Genoese, and he heard about it; knowing perfectly well what would happen once his wife were in his enemies' oily clutches, he sent Saint-Florentino back at top speed to stop her (it is not clear whether she would have fallen for the Genoese chicanery or, having enough experience of their wiles, declined the offer on her own account). Anyway, she and Antonio met and stayed in Aix-en-Provence.

The next trick the Genoese played was a foul one. They started to spread a rumour about Vannina and Saint-Florentino. By the time it reached Sampiero's ears it had acquired enough circumstantial detail to convince him that it was true: perhaps the length of time he had been away, plus the difference in their ages, helped to obscure for him Vannina's loyalty and devotion. Saint-Florentino was a young man, Vannina was still a beautiful woman: what would be more natural than that she was tired of waiting for him? The outcome would inevitably be tragic, because in his fierce code, a wife's infidelity was punishable only by death. In a lesser man who loved his wife, mercy might be excusable: but he was Sampiero Corso, the rock-hard, inflexible leader of his people. He knew that, whether the rumour were true or not, Vannina, his beloved wife, would have to die for the good of his cause: weakness in him now would be taken as a sign that old Sampiero was cracking up at last, and if so, where was Corsica?

He arrived in Aix, and brought Vannina and the boy back to Marseille. We can imagine his silence, his immobility of expression, on the journey, and, if she were unaware of the reason for it, poor Vannina's perplexity. In Marseille, in the privacy of their room, Sampiero told her that, since she had offended him, she must die.

'Since you are the only man who has ever touched me,' said Vannina, 'then you must be my executioner.'

Tenderly, Sampiero asked her for pardon. Then he took the silk scarf from her neck, and strangled her with it.

This story, which runs remarkably close to the plot of *Othello*, may well have filtered through to England and inspired Shakespeare, a couple of score years later. It's possible: at any rate it ranks pretty high, in my opinion, in the list of historical grand tragedies.

Sampiero then returned to Corsica and recommenced, with desperate energy, his struggle against the Genoese. For three years he fought them up and down the country, sometimes beating them, sometimes withdrawing into the maquis and the mountains. Finally the Genoese talent for treachery finished him as it had finished Vannina. By some trick he was lured into a valley near Cauzo, ambushed, and killed.

His son, incidentally, escaped to France, where he made good, becoming eventually Marshal of France and Governor of Aquitaine.

After about half an hour of devouring my lunch, watching small boats sculling about in the Gulf and people ambling about in the Place Foch, I happened to look up into the western sky and noticed a great ugly bank of sombre cloud out to sea. A storm on the way! The atmosphere had been stickily hot all day, so a storm seemed very likely. I decided to take a quick stroll round the old town, then get out into the country before the storm broke. There is nothing amazingly attractive about the old part of Ajaccio: it is a maze of narrow streets of tall old houses, all dismally dilapidated, squeezed in between the citadel, a utilitarian fortification on the point, and the new part of the town. There is the cathedral, a semi-classic, rather baroque cream-washed building with a dome, but that also is regrettably shabby. Probably it is not an exaggeration to say that the only establishment in the old town, not obviously uninsurable, is the house where Napoleon was born. This is distinguished from its neighbours by being in an important position on a corner, by a fresh coat of whitewash and by a flag over the front door. It is now, of course, a Napoleon museum. Even this shrine is not free from the frequent reminders that whoever designed Ajaccio's drainage system was either totally incapable or blind drunk or both.

Ajaccio is full of Napoleon relics: the birthplace-museum, of course, statues, busts, pictures and horrifying souvenir knick-knacks in every shop, names of bars, hotels, streets, squares. There is a probably apocryphal story that Ajaccio got its name from Ajax, the Greek hero. It's a wonder they haven't renamed it Bonapartio.

I trudged stickily back along the Cours Napoleon, where every café was still thronged with Saturday-afternoon drinkers. There was the dreary approach-road along the head of the Gulf, Ajaccio F.C.'s football ground, sundry railway yards and gas-works and so on, then a little hill (on a day like this even a little hill was sweaty) and then the country again, quiet and green. All the time that great looming storm-bank crept up into the sky: its misty fingers first spread across the sun like spider's-webs, then veiled it with a faintly translucent fog, then grabbed it and swallowed it. I passed by Ajaccio's airport and turned my back on the sea and the storm.

It was extremely hot. Sweat poured off me by the handkerchief-full, and each kilometre added another superlative to the thirst I was working up. Surprisingly I found a tiny wayside bar near a level crossing, tended by a small boy, and a vociferous dog. The boy was anything but vociferous and just stared at me while I gulped my drink.

A few more kilometres and a lot more sweat later I came to the beginning of the hills again, the River Prunelli and the village of Pisciatello. It was now entirely cloudy and dusk was obviously going to be earlier than usual, but the imminence of storm had retreated. There was no public water in Pisciatello apart from the river, which was too clearly the village drain, and I was on the point of carrying on, when I realised that there was quite likely no water further on either, and it might well turn into one of those nights. So I turned back, procured water from the very pleasant proprietress of one of the village's bars, and camped in a highly dubious place that broke at least three of my camp-site-choosing rules: it was quite probably someone's property, it was under trees (which is horrible when it rains) and it was much too near the river—those chilly wet mists in the morning.

The storm did not break and no one came to disturb me. Not intentionally, that is. It was sheer chance that Pisciatello just happened to be a check-point on the current Rallye de Corse, the competitors in which roared down one side of the river, crossed the bridge, screeched to the check-point, shouted, laughed and chattered at the umpires, revved like seventy-six trombones and then charged through their gears up the other side of the river, in endless succession, all night.

Chapter Five

THE WARM SOUTH

It may have been a dodgy camp-site, that one at Pisciatello, but I got away with it: no rain, no mist, and no trouble, apart from Motor Rally Insomnia. I suppose that may have been what made me walk half a mile along the riverside road before I realised I should have been going in the opposite direction. I made up for it by calling in at the village shop, where a young woman with yesterday's make-up on and hair dyed the wrong colour, sold me some bread (it may have been yesterday's bread, too) and told me she had never heard of Meta fuel. Meta is the French equivalent of Pypro, the solid fuel tablets which, set alight on a little metal stand, constituted my cooking facilities. I had no real hope that she would have heard of them, but there was no harm in asking.

It must have been intuitive wishful thinking that made me take the wrong road because the first seven miles of the right one were all uphill. The mountains in Corsica rise so sharply so soon you have only to travel a few miles to be in among them at once. The morning was sunny and from the long winding road there were plenty of opportunities to look back on the pleasant variegated green woods and meadows, bright pastures, pocket-handkerchief vineyards and scattered villages. There was no wind, and the atmosphere was still torrid: as the day progressed, so did the clouds over the sky. Presently a spatter or two of rain appeared. From the Col de Bellevalle (from which I was horrified to see that the road, instead of descending as usual from cols, went on up) I could see the whole of the Gulf of Ajaccio in a hazy mist, the town an indistinguishable sprawl along its side, the Îles Sanguinaires, the string of islands off the furthest point, apparently hanging in space between sea and air, there being no difference in colour between the two. The sea, far from its proper Mediterranean blue, was a sullen, inanimate North Sea grey. As usual, no ships were upon it.

There had been, in my opinion, far too much *up* about the

70

morning's proceedings, and it was not until I came to a little village called Bisinao that there was a bit of walking on the flat for a change. Bisinao sounds more like somewhere in the Philippines, but it was another of these tiny lost mountain oases, set about with terraced pastures hacked out of the wild fells: a dozen dignified stone houses, a tiny chapel, no shops and no bars. There seemed to be no valid reason why it was there at all, but it was lovely. Its people eyed me with undisguised but not unamiable curiosity, and returned my greetings with instant warmth.

Round a couple of corners, a slab of savage mountainside hid the village, and the road hairpinned round a lively stream. Below the road there was a green bank at present overlaid with chestnut leaves from the huge trees, and I paused. The weather was still uncertain, but I was running out of socks, so I stopped, made it a dhobey-afternoon, and camped there. It rained a couple of times but I washed my socks and my feet; there was a little traffic on the road, but for the first time since God knows when, there were no barking dogs.

This country to the south of Ajaccio is greener and easier on the eye than the raw, harsh cliffs and chasms of the great central mountains. Villages are just as infrequent and there is no more, or less, attempt at cultivating the steep hillsides, but for all that they must be as fertile as any in the island. Cork oaks, wild olives and eucalyptus grow to a considerable height everywhere: this is by no means a desert.

The usual contour-following routine, through silvery-grey-green forests of olives, dark oaks and russet chestnuts, brought me on a calm clear morning to Cognocoli-Montichi. I stopped at its fountain for a drink, and being attracted by the lazy serenity of the village, stayed for a sketch. The passers-by, while I was standing there like Patience on her proverbial monument, included three boys; these, after staring at me and passing a few questionable comments, walked on in the direction of the next village, Pila-Canale. As I was going that way myself I quickly caught up with them. They were in their early teens, I suppose: a tall, skinny, dark, tanned one, a short, cropped-ginger-haired, long-faced, freckly one, and the third between the other two in height, fresh-faced, with a big mouth and big ears. This latter fancied himself a bit. They asked me where I was going and why I was going there on foot, and Big Ears indicated quite plainly, without

actually saying so, that he would rather fall off the mountain
than undertake a journey any longer than from Cognocoli to
Pila-Canale, on foot.

'But,' I tried to explain, 'it's by far the best method of seeing a
country, wouldn't you say?'

Cognocoli

He reacted with the Corsican equivalent of 'Oh yeah?' The
other two chaffed him, and told me not to take any notice of him.

'Do you,' I enquired of the other two, 'live in Cognocoli-
Montichi, or Pila-Canale?'

'In Pila-Canale, monsieur,' they both said at once.

'We have just been visiting in Cognocoli,' explained the tall
boy, 'and are going home to lunch.'

'We do not say Cognocoli-Montichi, monsieur,' added Ginger, 'it is just Cognocoli. Montichi is the name of the district.'

I'm glad of that, the full name is twice as long as the village. Because I was English the boys were particularly interested to hear what I thought of Corsica. Big Ears, when my nationality was disclosed, said, 'Spik Ingleesh?'

'Naturally,' I said in it. 'Do you?'

But Big Ears didn't, he was just showing off again. Ginger said 'English? He hardly knows any French!' and there would have been a fight but for the fact that we had arrived in Pila-Canale. We passed a bar where the men of the village were sitting at tables in the sunshine, chatting and sipping their pastis, which made me think of Keats and his beaker full of the warm south. You could spend your life sitting at a bar like that, where the other side of the road drops away to the olive-covered slopes and a bright stream, the blue-green hills lie complacently in the middle distance like dozing cats and leave you, between two of them, a glittering blue triangle of sea to give you the satisfaction of knowing it is still there, if wanted. But who wants it when there are friends to talk and drink with, and the warm sun to ease your conscience about doing any work?

The boys guided me to a shop-cum-bar next to the one I have just described, and we all crowded inside. It was run by a very tiny and completely charming old lady, who first served the boys with their bottles of pop, then attended, with a smile but without vulgar curiosity, to me. The boys departed, and were replaced by a small thin-faced man about forty years old with black hair smoothed down. The tiny old lady indicated to him, while fetching one of my purchases from a distant part of the shop, that I was English, and he took an immediate interest. When, after I had finished buying my stores, I said that I would stop for a Casanis, the little man to my surprise insisted on paying for it. We sat down and at once were joined by a young fellow for whom another drink was supplied, and it turned into a good old Casanis session.

'I saw you,' the young man said to me, 'sketching in Cognocoli. I am interested, because although I am only a paint-seller and Pierre here is a painter of houses, we are both interested in the painting of pictures.'

They discussed the paint trade for a while, and we had another round. Then they returned to the subject of pictures, and asked me about the other places I had seen.

'Have you,' asked Pierre, 'seen the Îles Sanguinaires, at sunset? A pity. Yes, you see, because at sunset you can see them standing out black against the sea and sky. Such colours you never did see. . . .'

'That is right,' the young man agreed, 'it is a sight worth remembering, and worth painting.'

We moved out to the bar next door, to a table in the sunshine and the company of the Patron who was a friend of Pierre's. But delightful as it was to sit idly chatting, with the sun warm on our backs, Pierre and his friend had work to do. They got up and went, and I loaded up and left the village to find a place where I could sit and have lunch.

Before I had passed many houses I encountered in the road the ginger boy again. At his instigation I stopped at a grassy bank there and then. 'Stay here,' he commanded, 'and while you are eating you can talk with me.'

He lived, he said, just down the road, with his father, mother, sister and six brothers. While he was detailing their names the tall boy turned up: they were supposed to be on their way to school, 'but we are often late. Once more will not matter.'

I told them a little about England, and the difference in climate, and asked them if they liked living here in Pila-Canale. 'Oh yes, we love it.'

'In the winter it is not so good, but when summer comes it is wonderful, so hot. We go to the sea, it's not far—' He pointed to that distant blue triangle between the hills '—and swim. The water, when the summer is really hot, is most beautiful and warm.' Ginger's grey eyes shone with enthusiasm, and the tall boy was nodding, to confirm each assertion. Other children passed by, one of whom was obviously Ginger's younger brother.

'Here,' Ginger called to him, 'this is an English monsieur.'

This smaller facsimile of Ginger advanced, patent disbelief written all over him. 'All right, say something in English, then.'

I made a little speech in that language. The boy's eyes opened in wonder, he grinned, thanked me, and ran away to school, chattering excitedly with his pals. It gave me an idea.

'Look,' I said to Ginger, 'do you speak Corsican?'

'Of course, monsieur.'

'Well, will you write me some, with a translation in French? I've never seen any written down.'

'What shall I write?'

'Anything you like.'

I gave Ginger a piece of paper and my pen, and he considered it thoughtfully for a while. 'Monsieur, do you like Corsica, and our village, and all the countryside?'

'Of course. It is very beautiful.'

'Right then.' He started to write these words:

'A vo vi piagi a corsica. Touti est mutagi vi piagini. Touti i paiesi corsi vi piagini.'

Underneath he wrote, in French:

'All Corsica pleases you. All the mountains please you. All the Corsican villages please you.'

'Before you go, monsieur,' said Ginger, 'will you write something for us, in English, and hide it here so that we can find it when we come back from school?' I promised I would, shook hands with them, and they were gone. When I had finished lunch I wrote a little note on the back of a chocolate wrapper, and built a small cairn of stones over it there on the grass. I wonder if they ever found it.

To leave Pila-Canale I had to go back through it, on a lower level. The lovely old stone houses were perched all over the hillside, gorgeous with banks of purple bougainvillea over their balconies and terraces, bright geraniums and hibiscus at their doorways, cats sprawled asleep on their warm steps. Down I trotted, down and down past the genial villagers exchanging pleasantries over the backs of their donkeys, back into the olive-covered hillside.

It was all downhill now. Still sunny, but not too warm, the afternoon took me out of the mountains and away from the village. The prospect was splendid still, but the only people I met were one old man with a gigantic Old Bill moustache and a horse and a cart, and the occupants of the only house I had passed since leaving the village. The old chap standing by his garden gate was glad of a short chat, and his wife very civilly leant out of an upstairs window and asked me if I was thirsty. I thanked her but said I was not. This was a mistake, because it was another five kilometres, a full hour, and a very steep hill (up, of course) before I found any water.

I was back in the mountains again, after a dip into a river valley, and I had some late sunshine to dry my socks, a gentle, soft breeze to dry my tent, and bucolic peace.

But the moon had a ring round it. There is an old country saying about that particular phenomenon; if they are forecasting something unpleasant, country sayings are usually right. This one was no exception. The day started off well enough, it was

SOLLACARO

only from about mid-day that it began to deteriorate. I found myself climbing in the most amazingly circuitious fashion around the foothills of the next mountain mass, at one point looking back as far as Pila-Canale, a white splash unbelievably high in the hills, at another arriving almost back where I had started, overlooking the rough country where last night's camp had been.

After a long climb I came at last to Sollacaro, a charming village set in the prevalent fashion high on a mountainside, with a limb or pup called Calvese a little way below it, and a long drop to a small cultivated plain, the coastal hills, and the sea. The road twisted round in the centre of the village and zig-zagged back up the hill. I found quite a number of elderly people standing around in the streets, all of whom greeted me affably, and I got the usual considerate attention from the shop-people. One went to great lengths to establish that she hadn't any Meta fuel, nor anything like it. It was not that I had run out of the English variety, but I would before long, and had no wish to be caught without.

The bar I chose for my morning aperitif was not prepossessing, just plain uncomplicated tables and chairs in a long bare room with uncovered boards that creaked and groaned as though the whole place, if nudged, would tumble down the hillside. But even the scruffiest, poorest bar—which this one almost was—is a home from home when filled by the Sollacaro people I met there. I was reading the first newspaper I had seen in days when they came in, just a couple of them at first, an old man in a white cloth cap and a younger, of the middle age. It wasn't that they said anything deeply significant, or revealed exciting episodes of Sollacaro history, or anything but a general interest in and comment on the places I said I had visited. What I appreciated was their patent wish to make me, an outlandish stranger and a foreigner too, well outside the usual tourist season, feel welcome. They enthused over the natural beauties of their island, argued about whether La Spelunca was more beautiful than La Scala de Santa Regina, and recommended, once again, the Îles Sanguinaires at sunset.

When they had gone, the proprietress of the bar, yet another kindly old lady, gave me a drink on the house and enthusiastically listed the local attractions.

'Only six kilometres away,' she said, 'there is a prehistoric camp.' I had noticed the signs to this, but they pointed not only in the wrong direction but downhill, an accumulation of obstacles too much for the poor old Traveller.

'Also, there is a big house quite near that once was occupied by Alexandre Dumas.'

'Which one, père or fils?' But she didn't hear the question.

Sollacaro, which is another of those places I feel I must revisit some day, is on the northern side of a south-westerly range of hills. From the southern side, having sweated up to the col and lunched at a deserted stone hut, I could see all the way down to the head of the Golfe de Valinco and the seaside holiday town of Propriano on the other side of it. The length of the afternoon's travels, in fact.

In the centre of this inspiring prospect was a sharp rocky eminence on top of which were the remains, so worn down they were barely distinguishable from the naked rocks, of a small

stronghold called Castello della Rocca. Whether it has any bearing on this name or not I regret I cannot say, but just for the
record there was a Corsican hero of the mid-fourteenth century
called Arrigo della Rocca, who in the scramble for power between
Genoa and Aragon, momentarily grabbed it for himself, and
ruled his native island for a brief stretch.

On the hillside above the road, and facing the castle, were
the tumbled ruins of a convent, so overgrown and sunken into the
ground, it seemed, like the castle, to have become part of the
natural topography. Below it, on the road, as if to point the con-
trast between the needs of different eras, was a brand new house.
It was built tall and four-square, exactly in the old tradition, and
divided into three or four apartments. Some of its inmates, including one lovely little dark-haired girl who was the finest piece
of scenery since Ajaccio, were gathered for a mid-afternoon gossip
on the patio outside. So, in the streets of Olmeto when I got there,
was most of its population.

Olmeto was a larger edition of Sollacaro, Pila-Canale, Bocognano and the rest: it was a town, with more houses, a bigger
church, post office, town hall and school, and more bars. Still it
had the complicated system of stepways linking the houses, the
beautiful outlook over valley, hills and sea, the road running
across, never down the slope. No Clovelly-like steps for a high
street here. There were any number of mid-afternoon gossipers,
of all ages and sexes, with apparently nothing else to do, although
it was ostensibly a working weekday. Just beyond the town was
its second town, of chapels and mausoleums, covering nearly as
great an area as the town of the living. Here and there men and
women hovered in it, weeding, arranging flowers, watering
flower-beds, just standing in solemn meditation, in mystic Celtic
communion with the dead.

It was not till I had struggled down the meandering road to the
gulf that I noticed the evil-looking inky mass of cloud building up
over the sea, and the sun about to be engulfed by it. It occurred to
me that it would be a good thing if I found water and a camp-
site forthwith, and in the natural order of things I could thereupon find neither. With cramp in one foot and a blister on the
other, with no source of water in sight and the storm rearing up
out of the west, it was beginning to look like a long trek to Propriano, in pouring rain, with a hotel-bill in the morning.

Then, down on the flat stretch behind the beach, an aged Citroen with already four passengers, screeched to a halt beside me.

'Propriano? Hop in.' It was a squeeze, but we made it, and the driver took off like a drag racer. I commented on the approaching storm, to express my thanks.

'Storm? No, that's nothing, don't you worry. But why do you walk? Why not ride on the cars and lorries?'

I gave them some explanation, which they did not believe. Why not hitch-hike? Well, I don't know: perhaps because it is too fast, too easy. It would mean flashing through Pila-Canale and Sollacaro and missing those conversations and smells and sounds and maquis-blanketed convent walls. It would also mean being shaken to a jelly by lunatic Corsican drivers like this one.

Within a few traumatic minutes I was standing in the middle of Propriano; although the whole sky was overcast by a funeral pall, it had not yet begun to rain. A street fountain was handy, a general store was open, albeit Meta-less, and a long road led out of Propriano into fairly flat country. Propriano, as I have mentioned, is a seaside holiday town, and therefore full to overflowing with hotels, bars and restaurants. It has a summer ferry service to Ajaccio, a beautiful outlook to the mountains west of Olmeto over the gulf, and in season is probably an excellent place in which to stay and enjoy Corsica. Just at that moment I couldn't get out of it quickly enough. I hurried up the long straight road, glancing fearfully over my shoulder now and then at the black, menacing clouds, and at last spotted a bit of rough ground behind a new cottage.

I was just in time, the rain started as soon as I had put all my gear in the tent and crawled inside. There was a little thunder and lightning and an awful lot of rain, which persisted most of the night. It kept the dogs quiet, but nothing much else could be said for it because life for the next couple of days was difficult. An endless procession of heavy, ragged black clouds surged in from the sea, and progress deteriorated into a series of dashes for the nearest shelter when the rain lashed down too heavily for comfort. I followed the Rizzanese river, which was being dredged for silt, for several miles inland, noticing with appreciation sundry efforts being made along its banks to clear away scrub-land for cultivation. Below Sartène, which, high in the hills, had been visible for miles, there was as big an acreage of vineyards as I had seen in Corsica.

Between showers I plodded up the long twisting road to Sartène's eminence. About half a kilometre before the town, at a spot where the only shelter was a ludicrously inadequate tree, the worst rain of the day came bucketing down, bouncing back from the road surface and drenching my trouser-legs. Both my boots leaked by this time. I tottered into Sartène, water running off me, waded through the streets and found a self-service store.

Sartène is an ancient grey stone town, built in the customary Corsican style around and over a mediaeval fortress, tiny fragments of which crop up now and then in the fabric of existing houses. It is a high place, commands a wonderful view over the Rizzanese valley down to Propriano and the sea, and is worth a good many days of anybody's time. The weather, when I was there, did not do it anything like justice. The charming lady cashier at the store had the grace to apologise for it. 'You've had a fine tour, up to now, haven't you?' she smiled, then agreed with the older woman behind me that it was terribly cold, for the time of year. Maybe, I thought, but it'll be a great deal colder back home, right now.

I wandered Sartène's old streets for a while, looking for a shop likely to sell fuel of the description I needed, but without success, and as it was now about mid-day most of them were closing anyway. The main square of the town, where stood the war memorial all bedecked with flags and flowers because tomorrow was Armistice day, had a railed-off side opening to the steep-sloping hillside, for the enjoyment of the view. This would have been rivetting, no doubt, in clear weather, but as at the moment it consisted of a shaggy phalanx of dirty grey rain clouds, I dived into one of the square's bars. A plump young man poured the drink and seemed of the opinion I should be locked up. 'Why walk? Why not hitch-hike? It's much easier, and everyone would stop and give you a lift.' I tried, wearily, to explain, but as this well-fed blossom had obviously never found any need to walk further than from bar-door to car-door, he was not convinced. In fact, in view of current climatic conditions, I was not too sure myself.

'This gent,' said Fatso to a worried grey man who had just crept in, 'intends to walk all the way to Bonifacio.'

The dyspeptic countenance showed no signs of emotion. He

picked up a newspaper, said 'Why?' laconically, and disappeared into a dark corner of the bar.

Having read the newspaper myself and drained a couple of Casanis, I left the bar to the crowd of post-prandial coffee-drinkers and card-players who had by now filled it, and went on my way. Lunch was a cold and uncomfortable affair, and I was glad to leave the fine old town and head for the sheltering hills. From here to the sea, the most south-westerly coast of the island, was a fine confusion of hills and dales and streams, quite wild and practically deserted. The only village along the way, Giuncheto, at the end of its own long twisting uphill lane, was perched high on a cliff. In its lee I was glad to find a convenient grassy-banked stream, and stayed there. Showers were still so frequent that washing clothes was out of the question and even washing myself was too lengthy an operation to be completed all at once. I got as far as washing one foot, but another heavy shower came and I had to grab everything and hop back to the tent. Quite some days elapsed before I got round to washing the other one.

It was a foul night, but remembering that other old saying about rain before seven, clear by eleven, I took heart and set off down the road to the Ortolo river. Here were more definite attempts to wrest some arable land from the maquis, and more power to their elbow, I say. There were already several good pastures and vineyards and it just shows what can be done if you try. The 'clear by eleven' part of the adage was coming true, fractionally and with not a second to spare, but more because I was walking towards a band of clear weather than because the area behind me was clearing up. At the Col de Roccapina the sun shone and the sea, which was quite adjacent, was a respectable Mediterranean blue for a change. The snag was that it was flecked with white: white horses from the howling stiff breezes that nearly blew me off the Col. On a craggy promontory into the sea, near the Col, there was an old watch-tower, and behind it a curiously prominent rock-formation, in the likeness of a crouching animal: the Lion of Roccapina.

On the Col there was a solitary inn called Oasis de Roccapina. Oasis indeed it was, because there was not another habitation in sight; but huge notices about the place promised that soon there would be. 'Domaine du Lion de Roccapina' was another project to buy land on the narrow coastal strip and sell it off in lots for

building summer villas. The company perpetrating this outrage
on virgin Corsican soil was from the French mainland—and it was
not popular. On one notice, in large black letters, was scrawled
'Corsica wants to live', on another, 'No colonisation!' But like
most slogan-scrawlers in public places (most of Corsica appeared
to want Maître Tixier-Vignancour to be their next president)
they would undoubtedly be on the losing side.

I drank at the Oasis, and lunched in a sheltered spot in the sunshine just below the shoulder of the Col, in sight of Sardinia
across the straits.

THE LION OF ROCCAPINA

The southern shore of Corsica was a barren place: the wind
howled out of the west, sweeping over bare, bleak rock, maquis,
no trees, no houses, no cultivation. Just inland, in the vicinity of
Monaccia, there was a different picture, of pasture, vineyard and
a general appearance of agricultural endeavour, for a change. In
Pianotolli, a small village looking out to sea, I expected to find
nothing open, remembering last year's November the Eleventh in
Leognan, in Landes, when I was caught without any provisions
but half a bar of chocolate and a mouldy sandwich for supper and
breakfast. But everyone was in Pianotolli, and I found a shop
where two incredible old yellow, wizened, crow-like crones were
serving a group of gypsy lads. I was thirsty and sought a bar, but
surprisingly there weren't many. I tried the door of one and found
it locked, but as I moved away it opened and I found myself wel-
comed into it by two middle-aged ladies who were only too glad
of a chat with a stranger. It was a bar-cum-store, like the one in

Pila-Canale; I sipped a couple of drinks and answered their questions about my doings. Nothing fundamental transpired from our conversation, just general chit-chat, but we got on splendidly for *entente cordiale* and Anglo-Corsican relations, and at the finish they filled my water-bag, one lady gave me a raisin cake and the other a large bag of crisps.

Then when I was half a kilometre down the road I remembered I hadn't paid for the drinks: revenge, however unintentional, for Bocognano!

My last night, as it turned out, in Corsica, was disturbed only by rain, a snorting mule in the next field, chaps on motorcycles singing down the road, and more rain: apart from that it was quite peaceful. The day was reasonably clear, and the coast-road continued mostly straight and hilly. Occasionally it crossed the head of a lovely inlet, like an Irish creek; the Golfes de Figaro and Ventilegne were quite lovely, and totally devoid of human encumbrance. This coast was stony and barren, apart from the inextinguishable maquis, and there were no people and no animals. Just the grey-bodied crows common to all the land, and the gulls, a rare motorist, and me.

Apart from a glimpse as you top the last ridge of hills, you can see nothing of Bonifacio from that road until you get there. By the time I emerged from a sort of chasm and suddenly arrived at the harbour, it was raining again. The harbour is a natural one, cliff-locked and narrow. A row of houses, shops and bars sidles along one edge of it, towards a massive slab of cliff embattled with grey old walls which surrounded the citadel and main part of the town of Bonifacio.

I wish I had had more time to inspect Bonifacio, but the Tirrenia ship *Luigi Rizzo* was in the harbour, and the man in the Tirrenia office on the quayside was not sure if I would be able to obtain any Italian money if I postponed passage until the next day, a Saturday. The ship sailed at two-thirty, which left me half an hour, and I was tempted to stay, but the spectre of Corte breathed down my neck. No, it wasn't worth being in a strange land without money for two days. I bought a ticket, had a hectic whip round the shops, finding one at last which sold Meta, took in a final Casanis at the nearest bar, watched the sailors perilously loading cars aboard the *Luigi Rizzo*, then went aboard myself, along with a dozen or so others. I leaned over the ship's side and watched the two legionnaires on the quayside, a policeman or two, the customs men milling about, the two palm trees waving in the breeze before the customs house, the pretty girl hanging out washing from an upstairs window of the bar where I had just drunk, the friends and relations waiting to wave goodbye on the quayside, the old cobbled steps leading between the houses up to the bastions and the town.

There was not much more time before the *Luigi Rizzo* was pushing out into the heaving, tumultuous sea and we were looking back at the cliffs of Corsica, Dover-white, and with a great thunderous inky-black cloud-mass hanging over the mountains. I had not seen much of Bonifacio, but there is a good story about it and with it I will conclude this part of my travels.

In 1421 King Alfonso V of Aragon, trying to subdue the island preparatory to wresting it from Genoa, laid siege to Bonifacio. The siege lasted and lasted until Alfonso believed that the defenders could not possibly have enough provisions to hold out a day longer: he therefore called upon them to submit. But the people of Bonifacio were as stubborn and proud as any of their compatriots, and they were determined not to give in to any Spaniard. In point of fact they *were* pretty short of provisions, but clearly, it was necessary to convince Alfonso that they had plenty. So they collected all the remaining loaves of bread and, in full view of Alfonso and all his army, heaved them over the walls. Bread? Plenty of bread and some to spare. Then the women of the town collaborated in one of the most remarkable exploits of any siege. From their own milk they made a great cheese, and sent it by messenger to the King.

Alfonso was amazed. So much bread they could sling it over the walls, so much cheese they could send him some, they must have enough food in there to last for ever! He called off the siege, sailed out to sea, and was met by a relieving fleet of Genoese ships and chased away.

The *Luigi Rizzo* rolled and pitched and I looked back at the cliffs and the great cloud-covered mountains: Corse, la belle Corse, like a lovely, voluptuous, atavistic woman. Too proud to work, too sensitive to bother about commerce, capable of grand, savage passion, always willing to welcome a friendly stranger with a warm smile.

PART TWO

SARDINIA

Chapter Six

GALLURA AND LOGUDORA

I cannot give a detailed picture of Sardinia, because I went through it so quickly. I make no excuses for this, but there was a reason. I found out from the office of Tirrenia, the Italian shipping line, in Bonifacio, that there would be a boat to Tunis leaving Cagliari in one week's time, and another in three weeks' time. As things turned out it seemed more sensible to try for the first one, so that is what I did.

I missed seeing, probably, the best parts of Sardinia, so cannot describe them or recommend them. What I shall set out in the ensuing pages are my impressions of the parts, from the extreme north of the island to the capital, Cagliari, in the south, that I did see. Despite frightful difficulties with the Italian tongue, with which I am unfamiliar, I met and conversed with some interesting people and observed something of the state of the Sardinian people, which is rather dissimilar to what I have since read about in guide-books. Anyway, until I get to the Tunis part of my travels, where I met some people who at least spoke a language I understood, perhaps you will bear with me.

The *Luigi Rizzo*, which was small and painted white, was not exactly a blue-riband winner. The seas in the Bonifacio Straits were corrugated: one minute we were high on a crest, with a splendid prospect of the sky and the sunlit hills of Sardinia, the next it was replaced by a glowering wall of greeny-blue water and we all had that floating feeling in our stomachs. Impervious to this (and being the only representative of my traditionally phlegmatic countrymen, I had to pretend to be likewise) the man sitting next to me was pointing out excitedly to his companions the geographical points of the outlying islands as we approached them. There was a maze of small stony islands off this north coast, a confusion of crags, rocks and water rather like the Hebrides. Over an hour since we put out from Bonifacio we reached the shelter of a deep cliff-protected creek, and the *Luigi Rizzo* docked.

With our passports returned to us unmarked, and the customs, in a little shed, a farcical formality, I was looking around for a source of money-exchange: seeing there was an office at the quayside bearing some title involving tourists, I enquired there, with a carefully rehearsed phrase, and was lucky.

It was now getting on for four o'clock and a cold, fierce wind was blowing. I decided to go up to the town of Santa Teresa and find a cheap hotel for the night. That would give me time to find my bearings and begin to get accustomed to this totally strange land.

Santa Teresa di Gallura, the town's full name, lay sprawled on top of the bare sea-cliffs. Its houses were quite unlike those of Corsica: there were clay-surfaced side-streets full of plain single-storey cottages, colour-washed in pinks and greens. The larger places, in the main streets and in the square, were equally plain to the point of ugliness. On the edge of the cliffs and further down towards the beach were a number of big modern hotels, all stuccoed and colour-washed, and distinguished by series of rounded arches for windows, doorways and colonnades. Most of them, with their eyelid window-shutters down, were asleep for the winter, but I found one, looking out to the sea and the obscure sombre shape of Corsica from the cliff-tops, that was open and glad to welcome me as its only customer. Its presiding genius was a plump, amiable lady who listened sympathetically while I struggled with my phrase-book and eventually extracted from her the hour of dinner. Then I sauntered out to have a look around town.

It was a geometrical kind of place: all laid out in squares, with intersecting right-angled streets. Even the houses were square. There were no trees, no flower-beds, and not much fresh paint about. Plenty of people, mostly men, stood around in the streets and in the main square, staring at me as I passed them by. I was

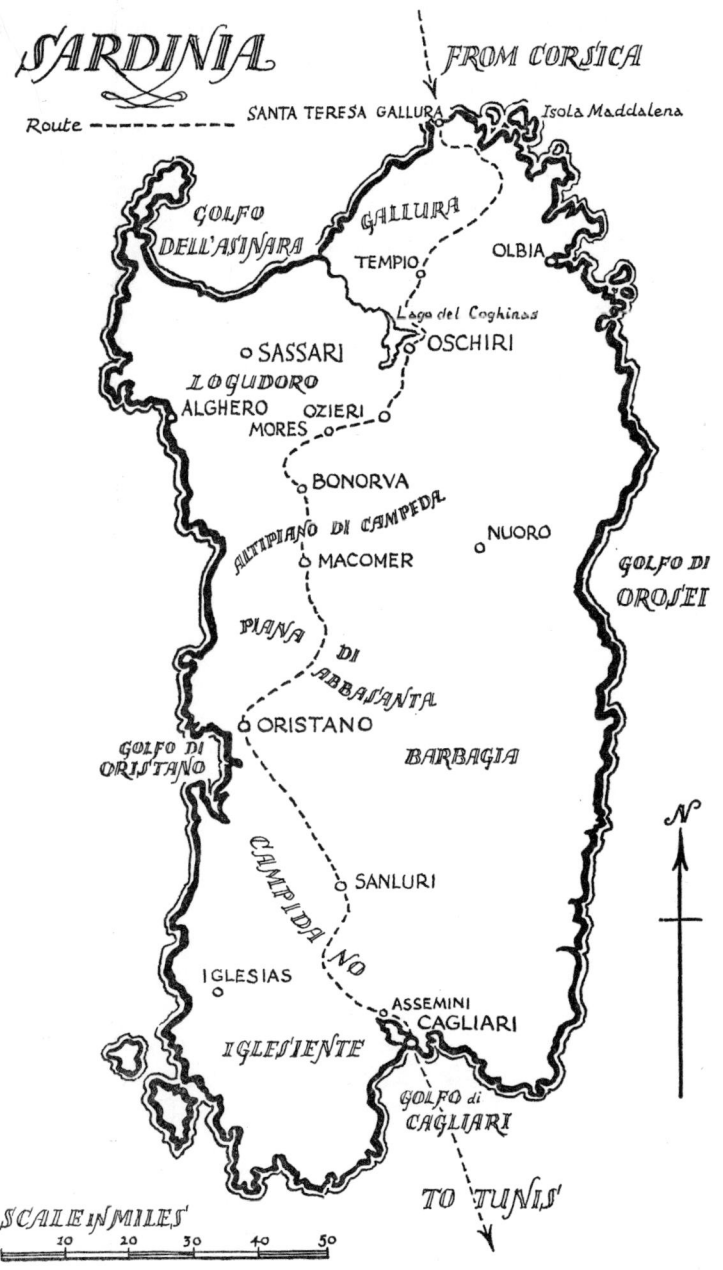

in need of a map of the island, having been unable to obtain one either at home or in Corsica, so I kept an eye open for a likely map-shop. There wasn't one. I bought some postcards, then went into one of the bars in the square. While I was sipping a Ricard, and trying to observe what the locals, at their tables in a dark corner, were drinking, I was joined by a thin, wiry man with thin, wiry hair and a yellow and brown patterned sweater. He spoke to me, and I soon discovered that he could speak French. He told me he was Genoese, and was working here. We exchanged inconsequential small talk, got friendly, and I bought him a drink (he only wanted orange juice).

'I have been trying to find,' I told him, 'a shop where I can buy a map of Sardinia, but have had no success. Have you any idea where I can get one?'

'Most certainly,' he said. 'When we have finished our drinks I will show you.'

There was a bookshop there in the square. I had missed it because there was no indication outside that it was a bookshop, no window-display, no sign. The doorway was screened, like most of the shops, by a curtain of coloured plastic strips, so you couldn't see inside that either. But although it was clearly quite a good bookshop, it had no maps of any description.

'Come with me,' said the Genoese, 'we'll go to the Tourist Office.'

'Not the one down by the quayside?'

'No, there is another, next to the Post Office.'

A little way from the main square was another square, in which stood the Post Office—a very elegant building—and the church, and a traffic policeman. The latter personage, in a light green, peaked-capped uniform and in need of a shave, was standing in the middle of the square. We approached him.

The Genoese explained what we wanted and introduced me. The policeman's placid countenance creased into a grin. 'How do you do?' he enquired, in English. He was really quite good at it, and we got on well. Unfortunately, he said, the Tourist Office was not open just at present. Why did we not try So-and-so's shop, it sold other things for tourists? We did (it was on the other side of the main square) but it did not sell maps. What about the other souvenir shop, in the square, the young woman there suggested? But it was closed.

'Never mind,' said the Genoese, 'it will be open in the morning.'

'I would never have thought,' I said, 'that it would have been so difficult to buy a map.'

'Yes, but you see Santa Teresa is a small town, and although everyone in it knows everyone else, out of the summer season there is seldom anyone else here, so there is no need for maps. I must be going home to dinner, now. Good luck!'

I shook his hand and thanked him for his trouble, and went back to the hotel. Dinner was mostly spaghetti; on television, which I watched for a while with the hotel people, the advertisements were just as stupid as ours at home.

Gallura is the name of the district in the north of Sardinia through which I journeyed all my first full day in the island. Topographically it is somewhat similar to the southern coast of Corsica: bare, windswept rocky hills, stony shores, scrub-covered fells, scarcely a tree in sight and the minimum of population. But whereas in Corsica there is not much more than a half-hearted attempt at taming the wilderness, here they at least have a go. Neat dry-stone walls encircle the stony pastures, where herds of smoky-grey and fawn cows graze, like darker Jerseys, and there are even fields ploughed and under crops. Farmhouses are more frequent, and although the place isn't lush with East Anglian prosperity, there is the general impression that the Gallurans do their best.

The people of Gallura have a reputation for hardiness, and pride in it, even among other Sardinians who are as tough a bunch as you will find anywhere along the Mediterranean shores. With an introduction to Gallura like the one I had, it was not long before I could see why they had to be.

It was a bright, windy morning; I had eaten everything in sight on the breakfast table, settled up with the kindly proprietress (the bill came to about twenty-six shillings, which is pretty reasonable in any language), laid in a few stores and set off along the wide, straight road that led inland. Quite soon I saw an Esso petrol station (*'Metti un tigre nel motore'*) and my map problem was solved.

Up on the heights behind the town the wind blew fiercely; the clouds were thickening and an ominous dull grey mass was building up in the west. The fine road, after striking boldly southward from Santa Teresa, gave up after a couple of kilometres and turned eastward along the coastline. The wind was behind me, and for a while I failed to notice the progress of the weather. I came to a point where I could see down into the harbour of Santa Teresa, its sheltered waters like a mill-pond compared with the choppy, thrusting seas outside. A few kilometres further on there was not a tree, nor a bush, nor a building of any sort, in sight, and glancing back, I saw the heavy blue-black thunderheads looming miles high, not a vestige of light on the horizon, and already the rumbling symptoms of a storm to end all storms.

Good Lord deliver us, I thought, this is going to be unpleasant. I hurried on, hardly knowing why, just feeling I should make all possible haste before the storm reached me. Oncoming cars, buffeted and bruised by the wind, were holding the road with extreme difficulty. The little Lambretta vans, so attractive in their economy, were almost at a standstill, lacking anything like the power to make way against the wind force. The low-flying clouds were already surging over the summit of the nearest hill, and the rumbles were nearer and louder. I jammed my hat hard down and pressed on desperately, up a slight rise and round a bend. Still no cover, not a thing, and the storm nearly on me. . . .

Then I saw a little hut, standing at the roadside.

I don't know whether granite blocks and proper slate roofs are the usual order for bus-shelters in Sardinia: I never saw another one like it. As far as I could see, this splendid refuge was built for no other reason than to provide relief, in a moment of dire need, for the poor old Traveller, who never thanked Providence more heartily than when he had hurried inside, sat down on one of the granite benches, and watched the storm break.

It was tremendous: thunder and lightning, a wind that blew the rain horizontally, blinding, stinging hail that bounced a foot high when it hit anything, all hell let loose. I settled back comfortably into the driest corner of my sturdy shelter and ate potato crisps and chocolate. In half an hour the worst had passed over, and a quarter of an hour after that the sun came out. I emerged and continued along the shining, steaming tarmac road.

But the wind was still high and there was apparently a limitless supply of dirty grey rain-clouds out there in the west somewhere. By the time I had reached a miserable village called Porto Pozzo there had been several showers and now a dreary, relentless drizzle, intensifying now and then into drenching rain. Porto Pozzo was on the shores of what would have been, in fine weather, a beautiful inlet in the rocky coast: a strip of sheltered water which in summer would be tranquilly azure and dotted with fresh white yachts, and was now grey, ruffled, cold and bleak.

The village itself was a wretched huddle of low plain buildings without much of anything to recommend them. Their beauty was hardly augmented by an incredible number of poles and wires. Whatever else they didn't have, I got the impression that every house, cottage, cow-shed, pig-sty and outdoor thunderbox, was fully equipped with electricity, telephone and television. I went into what I took for a bar, by the beer-ads outside, but which turned out to be a shop, bought some beer and stayed for a while, waiting for the rain to stop. Several lads from a nearby building site joined me, for the same purpose, and one of them speaking French obliged with some light conversation. I was really looking for some kind of shelter where I could have lunch, but the only thing available was the indifferently-roofed verandah of a hibernating bar-restaurant.

The rain, which had persisted steadily all through my lunch half-hour, lashed down like Niagara as soon as I set off afterwards. At the end of the village was a large, new, proper bar, where several people were gathered in some kind of horse-play under cover of a sort of patio. I made a dash for it. A hoarse-voiced, loud-mouthed, forceful type in an open-necked white shirt greeted me. He asked me a series of questions, and I was able to answer some of them. I tried to explain that I was supposed to be walking through Sardinia, but he failed entirely to understand why, and sneered at my inability to communicate with him in his own language. He gathered round him some of the other lads who were skylarking about, and said in a very loud voice words to the effect of: 'This fool is going through Sardinia, on his own, and he doesn't understand Italian. How stupid can you get?'

Just then, with the rain still bucketing down outside and the wind whipping up the water in the creek to white horses, I felt inclined to agree with him. But there was yet kindness in him. He asked me where I was going—that much I knew—and I said Tempio, which was a couple of days' march away.

'In that case,' said he, 'you have no need to worry. He—' indicating a young, blue-chinned fellow in a neat suit who was just beginning a hand-clasp contest with one of the others '—he is going to Tempio. He will take you in his car. Just you wait here.'

We crowded round and watched the contest: the two opponents were evenly matched and the struggle oscillated excitingly. Eventually the blue-chinned one, despite a scratch on his disengaged hand caused by bashing it against a wall, gained the upper hand and forced the other into submission. The onlookers made a terrific amount of noise all the time, foremost among them of course being the white-shirted one. I waited while the winner had his scratch treated by the lady of the house, then we left.

After a few more kilometres we left the coast road and headed inland, up a twisting valley road, which my driver negotiated with confident dash, to a Col, and then into a wide open plain. This was rimmed by low hills, and was partly wild and woody and partly cultivated. It may have been the weather, still wet, windy and dismal, but I thought the villages we passed through looked singularly unattractive, like Porto Pozzo. We took a short cut, along a side-road with an atrocious, unmetalled surface, through a village called Aggius that was large enough to have rated as a town in Corsica, and back to a T-junction with the main road. We stopped.

'There,' said Blue-chin with a smile, 'is Tempio, about a kilometre away.' We could see some of its houses, on a hill to our left. He was obviously going right.

It had stopped raining, but the wind was cold and more rubbish was threatening to pour over the green hills at the back of the town. Camping being too nasty to contemplate in such conditions, I resigned myself and a few thousand lire to another hotel. The choice was not large, so I settled for the first one I came to, a modern, clean place on the edge of the town: I think at that time of the year there was only one other open. When I had dumped my kit in a very smoothly furnished room with two beds (I assumed, since I had asked for one, that they hadn't a room with only one) I strolled out to take a look around town.

It was quite a while before I could locate the centre, the *raison d'être*, the hub of the place, because there was a maze of side roads and none of them seemed to lead anywhere but outwards. Eventually I tracked it down, and although the outskirts were anything but impressive, I rather liked Tempio proper. It was a close huddle of plain but dignified grey stone buildings, mostly with little wrought-iron balconies to the first floor. Several little places or squares separated these sardine-packed houses, and between two of them was the church. This was big, in the same dark grey stone, in the Roman style, with rounded arches and windows and a tall square campanile. Inside was the first real architectural beauty I had yet seen in Sardinia: simple classical pillars and capitals and the same Roman arches, but all beautifully decorated in fresh grey and white, the floor and all the statues and ornaments clean and polished.

Outside it was raining again, so I dived into a bar for shelter. Bars in Sardinia are also sweet-shops and often pastry-shops as well: the people seem to eat a great deal of pastry, lovely appetising cakes and buns with an immense variety of ingredients. I found that the longer I stayed in Sardinia, the less I was able to resist the temptation to sample two or three of these delicacies every time I passed a bar. But these were early days in Tempio and I hadn't yet formed the habit: I should have done because dinner was not until eight and it was a hungry wait. I had a Campari soda (about one and twopence: the cost at home is astronomical), waited for the rain to ease off, then found my way back to the hotel.

When I let myself into my room I thought I had let myself into someone else's. It looked like my room, but where was my gear? I had left it there, and now it was gone. I went outside to look at the door number again: twenty-four, that was the right number, so this must be the right room. Where, then, was my rucksack? I went down to the reception desk, where a different young lady had taken over, and put the situation in my incoherent Italian. Mystification was writ large upon the good girls's countenance. She looked up the register, and read out another name for room number twenty-four, not mine. Good Lord, I thought, this is like one of those spy stories: the next thing will be to produce the lad who carried my bag upstairs and he'll swear he's never seen me before. And then the police will arrive, and I'll find I've lost my passport. . . .

They did produce the lad who carried my bag upstairs. And he grinned all over his amiable face and led me upstairs again to another room, a single room, to where they'd moved my kit.

'It was a single room you wanted, Signore? Well then, here you are. It was not a double room you wanted, at all, was it?'

It was a perfectly good room, and furthermore it had a radiator that actually worked, so I had dry socks and boots in the morning. I cleared off everything edible on the breakfast table again, removed a few more thousand lire from my wallet, and went.

Tempio—the full name is Tempio Pausania—stands on a spur of the Limbara Mountains, which range separates Gallura from the rest of Sardinia. They are not nearly as high as some of the Corsican monsters I had been accustomed to, but a pretty considerable lump of rock nonetheless, and in order to get south to Oschiri and beyond, I had to go into and through them. I was therefore quite glad to accept a lift from a little dark man with a small son, who said he was going a few kilometres, which were mostly uphill, in that direction. We drove up the side of a green pleasant valley, with farms on its bottom, but before we reached the Col at the top we stopped, I baled out, and my late benefactors turned off down a frightful track to a village.

On the other side of the Col, called Passo del Limbara, was a deeper, steeper V-shaped valley, even greener and even more pleasant, especially since the sun now came out and I felt warm, for the first time since landing in Sardinia. The road wound along the side of the valley, as roads did in Corsica, but this was a much better road than any I had encountered there. Better for motorists, anyway: the steep banking and camber at every corner may have been fine for them, but it was ankle-straining stuff for the poor old walker—not that anybody does much of that in these parts, if they can help it.

Where a bright splashing stream burbled under the road and tumbled down into the valley, I stopped for a sock-washing session and lunch. By the time I was ready to move again, the wind was colder and there was a hint of trouble about the weather. At the end of the valley there was a low ridge, and beyond it a long and handsome lake, called Lago del Coghinas, and beyond that, the loveliest sight I had yet seen in this curious land. It reminded me of the background to an Italian Renaissance painting, one of those long-distance, bird's eye views of rolling, sunlit wooded hills and fresh green pastures, the flash of water here and there and the overall feeling of Elysium about it. Beyond the lake the rounded hills, snoozing in the gentle sunshine, mingled and blended into a harmonious pattern with the nearer, brighter shades of green, the oaks and olives, the occasional poplar, the sheep-pastures. This, I felt, was what Sardinia ought to look like: serenely beautiful.

The only thing that tended to spoil it was the drought of the lake; instead of sparkling blue water from rim to rim, there were huge expanses of sand and mud on either side, and what water remained was a depressed muddy brown. It was more like the Thames estuary at low tide than a fresh-water lake in Sardinia. Which, I thought, was odd considering the amount of rain that we had been blessed with in the last week or so.

I crossed a bridge at one end of the lake which, standing high above the water on long, exposed stilts, looked rather ridiculous. There was nothing ridiculous about the fresh lot of dark storm-clouds that were building up over the hills to the west. What, still more? Couldn't it stay fine for more than four hours at a time? I started looking apprehensively for water and a possible camp site, before the storm arrived, but all the watercourses were dry (significant à propos the lake) except for one miserable trickle. It didn't look too healthy, but I couldn't afford to be fussy. Then it appeared there were fields and orchards, all fenced off, either side the road, and nowhere feasible for a tent. The storm approached, and the rain started; a man standing at the roadside under an enormous green umbrella grinned at me and said cheerfully, 'More rain coming!'

The wind whipped up to gale force, the sky blackened, thunder mumbled across the hills, the rain eased off, showered, came on again, eased off again. There was nothing in the way of shelter about, the only trees were silly little saplings, but there was a stone wall between the road and the storm. I squatted down beside it and retreated behind my cape, which normally served as a groundsheet. The man with the umbrella waved at a passing bus, which stopped for him. I had the storm to myself.

However, it wasn't a patch on yesterday's effort: it thundered a lot and rained more, but without the diabolical malevolence of the other, which was just as well since I was wet enough as it was.

All the fields were walled off: there was nowhere that wasn't.

I decided to risk being thrown out, hopped over a wall and camped in someone's field, a bush-grown, thistly patch with a fine view of a green, moist valley beyond the shining and steamy road. When I was set up and in the middle of supper, a small dog trotted up and barked indignantly at me, and it was followed by a man. He, a stocky, unshaven individual in a cloth cap, rubber boots, and a green umbrella slung over his back, appeared to be the owner of the field. I expected trouble, but after a good deal of talk on his part and 'Non capisco' on mine. I gathered that he was only concerned in my welfare and was suggesting that I should go up to his house with him and sleep there for the night. He didn't in the least mind me being there. I refused as graciously as my Italian would permit, and we parted on excellent terms, which is more than could be said for his dog. That officious wretch came at intervals during the evening and snuffled and barked all round the tent.

It was a dreadful night, but a bright and sunny morning; at seven the owner's father, also cloth-capped, rubber-booted, green-umbrellaed and unshaven, came to enquire if I had slept well and had not been too cold. I was enormously impressed with the benevolence and courtesy of these country people.

I ambled down to Oschiri, rejoicing in the rare sunshine, although the wind was still vigorous. Oschiri, in the middle of a wide plain, may have been remarkable for something, but it was not beauty. Its houses were small and drab, and its church, a miniature imitation of Saint Peter's, possessed a dome in such an offensive red, it cancelled whatever aesthetic qualities it may have had. Quantities of people thronged Oschiri's streets, and I discovered it was market day: stalls were set up and doing good business on a waste plot in the middle of town. Most of the women were dressed in black, and even the younger girls wore a black shawl, a corner of which they would hold up to cover half their faces. Whether this was as protection against the cold wind or plain modesty I cannot say; since they did it whenever I approached and leered at them, it was probably the latter.

Out of town I passed a military camp, two cheerful motor-bike policemen, and a level crossing, on the long drag back up into the hills. Traffic was not heavy. Among it, on their way to market, were an ox-team, cart and driver, and a farmer on horse-back. The oxen were the smoky-fawn breed prevalent hereabouts; the cart was of a pattern constant through countless centuries, a simple wooden contraption with huge solid wooden wheels. The driver strolled by the side of the slow plodding team, waving at them spasmodically with a long whippy stick; the regular, monotonous rumble and plod reminded me of the cart Moussorgski dreamed up for one of his Pictures at an Exhibition. The horseman, dressed mostly in corduroy, plus the statutory cloth cap and six-day stubble, had so laden his animal that there was more bulging sack than either horse or rider.

Road and railway, crossing each other with astonishing frequency, followed a lovely green river valley up to the Plain of Ozieri. One peculiarity of this country that puzzled me was the occurence on occasional hilltops of round towers, all ruinous, in a dull reddish stone. Notices pointing to them would call them Nuraghe Sant' Abba Salida, or Nuraghe Santa Cherina, or some such thing. Nuraghe: I couldn't imagine even how to pronounce it, let alone what it meant, and according to my map, there were hundreds of them, all over the island. As it turned out, I didn't have to wait long for an explanation: the answer came that same day.

The Campo d'Ozieri was an enormous plain, stretching for miles, almost devoid of trees but all green and cultivated, dotted with occasional white farmhouses and hemmed in at the furthest rim by level-topped hills. One hill, higher than the rest, was completely flat-topped, like the MacLeod's Tables, in Skye. While I was pausing by the roadside to contemplate this phenomenon, a tiny little Fiat halted beside me and a cheerful young man in it offered me a lift to Ozieri. He was a mechanic of some description, dressed in blue overalls, a good-looking lad with straightforward blue eyes: I don't know if he was in love, or a habitual optimist, or come into a fortune recently or what, but he sang and whistled and made what conversation he could all the way to Ozieri. The flat-topped mountain, he told me, was Monte Santo (the Holy Mountain) and there was on the very top a most beautiful church.

We left the plain and started in between a couple of hills, and there in a cleft of them was Ozieri, all on end. We parted at the bottom, he went one way and I started to walk up the other, a zig-zag road that skirted the town's perimeter. From it I could see right across the cleft to the rooftops, towers and domes and was

not over-impressed with what I saw. There was something basically sullen about these towns, as though the people had enough
to do keeping life and soul together without sparing energy for
aesthetic considerations. The grace and dignity and easy leisure
of the Corsican towns was missing here.

I lunched in a small tree-shaded park affair at the top of the
hill, where lovers met for a lunchtime walk and families tumbled
around benches, then pressed on to the Mores road, without
troubling Ozieri any further than to call in at a bar for a drink
and some cakes.

The Mores road ran along a river valley whose bottom was
neatly tilled in market-garden strips, and further on in small fields
hedged with prickly pear. I had to laugh at one of these fields:
there was a modern tractor with a hydraulic two-furrow plough
working one half, and a chap stalking behind an ox-team, har-
rowing the other.

It was shortly after this that I met Luigi and started to learn
something about Sardinia.

It was a tremendous piece of luck being picked up by him, because I not only had the privilege of being transported through an
extremely interesting part of this Logudoro district, but had it
explained to me as well: and Luigi spoke French, so that even I
could understand what he was saying. He was a schools inspector, a young man of thirty or so, small, neat, with a thin, intelligent face and keen dark eyes, and black hair short and stiff, like a
broom-head. I was his second passenger, the other was a burly
red-faced countryman, again in the customary cloth cap and six-
day stubble.

'I am going to Bonorva,' Luigi said. 'If you like you can come
with me: it's about forty kilometres.' That was a day and a half's
walk, and meant that in the three days I had been in Sardinia I
would have travelled as far as would take me a week by just walking. It was then I realised that, at this rate, I would be advised to
try for the earlier boat from Cagliari. There had been someone
offering me a lift every day so far, without asking, and my Italian
was so bad I could never refuse convincingly or graciously.
Accepting was easier.

We drove through another enormous plain, close to the shoulder
of Monte Santo, with the church on its flat top. It was very odd,
but nearly all the hills encircling the plain also had flat, or at least

extraordinarily level, crests, as though some primeval giant had come along with a scythe and mowed them all off. We approached the village of Mores, whose church tower was huge, a tall square Byzantine structure surmounted by a gigantic statue: I commented on this.

'Would you like to visit the church?' Luigi asked.

'Very much, if it is not inconvenient to you.'

He parked the car in the small space before the church door, and we all piled out. Several poorly dressed countrymen standing and sitting about the church porch greeted Luigi and his passenger affably, and the latter stayed outside to chat with them. Luigi and I entered the church.

It was like an underground cavern, there was hardly any light at all: just enough to alleviate the sombre gloom, crawling half-strangled through a few tiny leaded windows high in the walls. After a few minutes' myopic peering, our eyes became accustomed and showed us details of the ornate decorations. It dawned on me suddenly, when I could see more clearly, that richly adorned though this interior once had been, now it was wretchedly shabby. Paint peeled dingily off the walls; statues and pictures, their colours faded to an indistinguishable anonymity, clothed them like the heterogeneous rags of a tired, dirty old tramp.

'I was in Tempio the other day,' I said, 'and the church there was beautiful inside, freshly painted.'

'Yes, but you see Tempio is a rich town. Mores is very poor; there is no work and no money, and no young people left. They all emigrate, to Italy, France, Germany, America and so on. Mores is poor in everything.'

Outside, blinking in the light, I could see what he meant. Houses in Mores, as plain as any I had seen, were shabby to the point of squalor. There are villages in Corsica, and Provence for example, which are devoid either of paint or of any signs of recent repair, but instead they have an air of sunny, indolent complacency, as if every day of the week was a Sabbath and to make any effort to mend your roof or paint your shutters would be a criminal act of desecration. But here it went deeper: something worse than poverty, worse than apathy. Mores had lost its last trace of dignity, and become a slum.

Disturbed and saddened by this, I climbed back into Luigi's

car, and found that I was now sharing the back seat with a lamb, in a sack, which belonged to the thickset farmer in the front. Both of these left us at another village further along, and I joined Luigi in the front seats.

We were still in the plain, the vast, faintly sheep-stippled, flat, treeless plain, hemmed at the edges with headless hills. There was one of those sand-castle round towers away to our left, in the fields, quite a big one.

'You see that tower, there,' said Luigi, 'do you know what it is?'

'No,' I said. 'I've seen some like it, though.'

'It's a Nuraghe.'

'There are hundreds of them marked on the map. What are they?'

Luigi stopped the car and turned it round. 'Come on, let's go and have a look at it, and I'll tell you about them.'

We drove down a side road towards the tower. It rose out of a mass of thick walls, and foundations of walls, and tumbled remains of walls, all built of huge blocks of dull brown stone. It was about the height and shape of a Martello tower, but it was obviously much older. Just how much older shocked me rigid.

'The Nuraghi,' said Luigi, 'were the dwelling-places of the ancient Sardinians, about two thousand years before Christ.'

Two thou . . . 'Then they're nearly four thousand years old!'

'Yes, that's right,' he said calmly.

'But this looks in better condition than many Roman buildings, and they're nearly two thousand years old.'

Luigi smiled: the crux of the problem was coming soon, I felt sure. We walked round the outside of the encircling wall, in and out of a series of curious circular foundations, all of this reddish-brown stone. 'No one knows for sure quite what these were,' said Luigi, 'but we think the whole place was a sort of fortified town. The tower there, and the walls round it (and inside there are a lot of rooms and chambers) as a military stronghold, and perhaps the living quarters of the chief, and these round things the houses of the people.'

'But what I don't understand, is how on earth it has stayed in such an unbelievably good state of preservation.'

Luigi slapped the topmost stone of the low wall over which we were climbing. 'Look at this stone. Examine it, closely.'

It was peculiar stone, now that I looked at it. Not like ordinary stone, which is solid and slab-like and impenetrable. This had little surface knobs, and fissures, and round holes, as if it had been fused together by artificial force of some kind. It reminded me of gigantic lumps of clinker. The answer began to occur to me, but I looked at Luigi for confirmation.

'Yes, it's volcanic,' he said. 'You see all these hills around us with flat tops? they're extinct volcanoes.'

'Like Monte Santo?'

'Yes. Volcanic rock is so hard it never erodes, never wears away. That's why the Nuraghi have lasted so long. Look at this: that's ordinary stone, and it's worn away almost to nothing.'

NURAGHE
DI S. ANTINE

It was the stub end of a Doric column, in a pale cream stone. 'This is Roman, isn't it? Did they use the Nuraghe as a fort?'

'That's right. Look, here is another column. They built their own extensions to the original structure, but look which has lasted the longer!'

'It's magnificent.'

'Yes. This one, Nuraghe di San Antine, is one of the best, but there are many, many others.'

We returned to the car and drove back to the main road.

'This plain,' said Luigi, 'is terribly poor.'

'Why? The soil doesn't look too bad.'

'There's no water. It's green now, because there has been rain lately, but in the summer it is so dry that nothing will grow. All the farmers, who had been here for generations, have had to leave. Sardinia is a very neglected country, you know. No one has ever wanted it enough to make it prosperous.'

'What about the Romans?'

'Oh, the Romans. You know what they were like: they came and took and took and put back nothing. So with every other colonising power. The Byzantines took over after Rome fell, then Pisa and Genoa, then Aragon, and finally Piedmont. Not one of them ever thought of putting back into Sardinia some of the money they had taken out: like a field that has been cropped and cropped and not fertilised, Sardinia has been spoiled by centuries of exploitation. It's not too bad now, under Italy, but we are still way behind the times, and still desperately poor.'

'You are Sardinian yourself, then?'

'Oh yes, and I'm very proud to be. You must realise, that by just going through Sardinia, and not knowing the language, you cannot hope to know much about the Sards. You have to go right into the remotest country villages, and talk with the elders, properly to know them. These places like Alghero, Sassari and Cagliari, they're not really Sardinia, they're full of tourists and foreigners. It's in places like this, and especially in the Nuoro country east of here that you meet the real Sards. The Nuoro people are strong, hardy simple folk—'

'But proud?'

'Yes, proud. I love them, and I love the island.'

Still in the lee of the old, dead volcanoes, we turned off the main road by a large house painted pink, called Casa Cantonieri—'they're for workers on the roads'—and Luigi stopped the car.

'I'm going to Bonorva, to visit the school. You can come with me into town if you like, it's only a kilometre up the road. The Cagliari road is up this hill, there.'

I told him that I would like to find, before too long, a source of water and a place to put my tent. 'Anywhere, so long as it isn't someone's property.'

He laughed. 'No one bothers about that in Sardinia. You could camp anywhere you wanted, no one would mind.'

On the way down the road to Bonorva Luigi stopped again and asked a passer-by for a suitable place where I could camp. The man indicated a nearby path up the hillside. 'You don't want to be too far away from people and houses,' Luigi said, 'in case you are bothered by hooligans.'

In Bonorva, whose houses, although as depressed and shabby as any, were more stylish than most, the whole population seemed to be doing nothing but standing on the street corners and staring. When Luigi and I had parted and he had gone off to his school, I went and had a look inside the church. I was expecting it to be like Mores, but it was large, airy and spacious, light and clean, and I was glad.

Ignoring the stares of the street-corner throng, I pottered off back up the street, past the battered old houses clinging to their wrought iron balconies as the last shreds of respectability, back to a fountain I had noticed at the roadside just outside the village. I found the footpath that Luigi's informant had recommended, and climbed up a steep hillside spasmodically planted with fig trees, fruit trees, cabbages and vines, looking for a flat bit. There wasn't one, so I pitched on a slope just slightly less hectic than the rest, much to the indignation of a silly little white dog which barked its head off but kept at a safe distance. There were any number of dogs barking that night: there were also moaning donkeys, tinkling cow and sheep bells, traffic, trains and a very cold icy breeze, to augment the possibility of rolling down the hill.

Very early history is for the most part a series of hypotheses. The Nuraghi were built in the Bronze Age, or possibly the Iron Age, we are told. Fair enough, that covers five hundred years or more; Luigi mentioned 2000 B.C., but it appears that in the fifteenth century B.C., a people called the Shardana, from Africa, arrived with their legendary leader Sardus, and settled in the south-west of Sardinia. So did *they* build the Nuraghi, or did their predecessors in the island? And if it was the latter, who were they anyway? No one seems to know anything about them. We know that after the Shardana, who obviously gave their name both to the island and all its subsequent inhabitants, there came Balari from the Iberian peninsula (Balearic Islands, yes?) and then Iolesi from Greece, and they settled in various parts, and then the ubiquitous Phoenicians rolled up and set up a trading post or two, the biggest of which was Karalis. But in those early days of commercial empires in the Mediterranean, when take-over bids came as thick and fast as they do in Big Business today, you needed power to back up your claims. The biggest fist had the best chance of winning the trade battle: Carthage replaced Tyre and Sidon, the Phoenician cities, and pretty soon their emporia were set up where Phoenician shop-fronts had been. They landed in Sardinia, knocked out Karalis, which was where Cagliari is now, drove the remnants of the Balari and Iolesi into the northern mountains, and settled in the fertile Campidano plain, in the south-west.

The Carthaginians never really colonised the island properly. The ball was sent rolling by the power-hungry Romans, and it went on rolling for a thousand hopeless years, with only a few minor deflections. In the middle of the struggle between Rome and Carthage, between the First and Second Punic Wars, Rome took over the island. The Sards, that curious amalgam of African, Spanish, Greek and numerous other people, took exception to Roman presumption and fought for their lives. In 175 B.C. the execrable Tiberius Sempronius Gracchus ordained a ruthless massacre of the unfortunate Sards and transported thousands of them back to Rome as slaves. To replace them he added another ingredient to the Sards' ethnological mixture by planting a vast number of Jews, a good many of whom probably died of the malaria that periodically removed a percentage of the island's population.

There are parts of Sardinia that even the Romans never managed to conquer. They called the mountain people Barbarians, and there is still a district in the central mountains called Barbagia. However uncertain their origin, as Sards they battled spiritedly against successive imposers of iniquitous taxes, and like their Corsican neighbours, their history is a long series of bloody rebellions and even bloodier reprisals.

No wonder Luigi and his mountain Sards are proud.

Chapter Seven

CAMPIDANO AND CAGLIARI

Bonorva in the morning was lively and animated: a great coming
and going of donkeys, horses and ox-carts, all tended by swarthy
Sards in brown corduroy. There were women in black, to-ing and
fro-ing with buckets and bundles balanced on their heads, and
the same throng of fellows of all ages standing about in the streets
and on corners. Moustaches were quite popular with this
crowd, and it appeared that anyone old enough to need to shave,
never did so more than once a week.

The day had started off well by being bright and sunny (it had
been a very cold night) and when I was folding up my tent and
putting it away I had a visit from the chap who lived in the
house at the top of the slope, the owner of the silly little white
dog. He was extremely pleasant (I am sure by now I have no need
to refer to the state of his chin) and I think he told me that if he
had known I was there he would have asked me up to sleep in the
house. Such a cold night, was it not?

Having located, with the help of some of the bystanders, a
general store which sold, among other things, bread, I found
in it a man who spoke French. He was suspicious of me at first
because he thought I was looking for work, but when I explained
that I was just passing through—nobody normally passes
through Bonorva since it's off the main road—his long, grave face
softened slightly and he managed a smile. He also managed to
allay the curiosity of all the other people in the shop, who thought
I was an escaped lunatic, at least. When I had finished buying
things, I asked him about the people standing around outside,
although I suppose I knew the answer already: but there were so
many of them!

'Oh, this is a bad time of the year. This is a poor village, and
there is no work. You see there is only the land, and most of that
is pastoral, so in the winter there is absolutely nothing for them to
do.'

It was the same everywhere I went in Bonorva: people stared, as if unable to believe their eyes, but when addressed with their own courtesy, would smile and respond amicably.

I walked back along the lane to the main road at a fairly brisk pace, overtaking on the way an ox-cart piled sky-high with straw bales. From the top of the long zig-zag climb up the hill on the Cagliari road, I could see the naked, lonely landscape, the dark soil of fields patterning the valley bottoms. All around were the level-topped hills, where the giant with the scythe had been. There was scarcely a tree in sight.

The hill I had climbed was the scarp slope of a high plateau which stretched like a moor as far as every horizon. Its scrub, rough grass and bracken were grazed by a large number of sheep and a few cattle and otherwise nothing disturbed the peace except for ruddy great trailer-pulling lorries that charged noisily past now and then. Funny things, whereas every other vehicle had left-hand drive in the ordinary way, all these heavy lorries were propelled from the right-hand side of the cab, as if they had been imported wholesale from England. This was not the case, as seen from their makes, so I suppose there is some Italian by-law regulating it.

It was not long after lunch, and less after a short chat with two soldiers changing the wheel of their jeep, when one of these vast slab-sided transport wagons hissed to a halt beside me and its occupants invited me aboard. They would, they said, take me to Macomer, and offered to go on to Oristano, but this would have been exceedingly uncomfortable because the cheerful thick-set driver's mate, in dark glasses and atrocious teeth, had given me his seat and was squatting on the engine cover. More than ten miles of that and his trousers would be on fire.

This high moor was called Altipiano di Campeda. Macomer (which should be in Scotland) was on the edge of it, before a sharp drop from the hills to a gigantic plain, all green grass and low stone walls, and completely flat, called Piana di Abbasanta. Several more Nuraghi stood on gaunt hilltops on its borders.

Apart from its position, with that splendid prospect across the plain and the wild moors behind, there was nothing particular about Macomer to distinguish it. The architecture was not inspired and neither was it in the least picturesque. Which was a pity, because with a little more charm and a touch of that old

Italian genius that made Venice and Florence, it could have been a place everyone would wish to visit.

I had in mind a visit to a bank for some money, buying a few postcards and writing them over a red wine or two. As it turned out all I could manage was the red wine part because everything except the bars was closed. The wine was a bit rough, but for about sevenpence the quantity was amazingly generous. I waited until two o'clock, expecting things to open then, but

BORORE

nothing did so I gave up and left. There were plenty of bystanders about, staring unsmilingly at me, and a swarm of schoolgirls who giggled and whispered to each other in that irritating way they have. The sun was shining placidly on the plain and from the edge of the town I could see where the road, leaving the hillside, ran straight as an arrow into the blue-green distance.

Down on the Piana I found a spring of water and camped early in a field near a village called Borore. I sat on one of those ancient lumps of volcanic rock, from which all the field-walls had been constructed, and watched the late afternoon sun making patterns of pale light and shadow on Borore's rooftops, and the dome of its church, and the crumpled cloth-folds of the mountains bordering the plain.

It was bitterly cold that night. The tent was saturated in the morning, but not by rain; but the day showed every sign of being fine again, which made up for sleeping in a deep freeze. I went at full speed along the ten kilometres to Abbasanta, in order to get there before lunchtime closing, passing through an occasional meagre forest of cork oaks and over one or two rivers, which were practically dried up. I found Abbasanta behind the railway, and as it appeared to be the usual collection of dreary one-storey cottages I did not examine it too closely. I visited a grocery for some stores, and made the day for the group of women assembled there and the pretty girl behind the counter by giving them something to talk about (I got the impression I was the first tourist ever to pass that way); then I had a couple of red wines in the bar next door, where there were more flies than customers. However the barman was interested and helpful, and after verifying that the Post Office would be closed by now, he told me I could buy stamps from the railway station, which sounds illogical but was perfectly true.

The character of the plain had not changed much all day, and the afternoon's walking was not too interesting, except for a Nuraghe by the wayside in the customary inconceivably good condition, until I fell in with a couple of teenage lads walking back to their village of Paulilatino. They were deeply concerned that I, a foreigner, should take home with me a good impression of their part of Sardinia: they praised its beauties, hoped that I had taken good notice of the Nuraghe I had just passed, and recommended Paulilatino for my attention as the most remarkable village in the island.

As we walked along one of them paused to gather some berries from a wayside bush, and offered them to me. They were small and blue, and I had seen them before and given them a wide berth on suspicion of poison. I was justified—they were ghastly. The lads said they were mirta, which I take to mean myrtle.

'Sometimes,' they said, 'they are quite sweet.' They must be an acquired taste, because I am convinced they were serious since they actually ate some themselves.

Paulilatino may not be the most remarkable village in Sardinia, but it was certainly more interesting than most I had seen so far. The houses were built of volcanic stone, with thick white mortar lines in between the courses: not only the old houses, but new ones too, and I was struck with the thought that this stone, so old, so tough and erosion-proof, had probably been used over and over again for house and wall-building, and would continue to house generations of Sardinians as it had, ever since there were Sardinians.

As usual, there were throngs of people about, and ancient women sat outside their cottage doors with spindles, spinning woollen yarn. A bit livelier, this village, a bit more self-respect, less of the apathetic squalor of others I had seen.

There were no more villages marked on the map until Oristano, so I watered up in Paulilatino and planned to stop in three quarters of an hour or so. However, I had scarcely put a kilometre between me and the village when I came upon one of those odd little Vespa pick-up vans, laden with gas-bottles. The driver was having a long discussion with a motor-cyclist, at the side of the road, but as I trudged past he noticed me and waved. As possibly everybody knows, the Italian gesture meaning 'come here' looks like 'goodbye', and you have to get used to this. I crossed the road to them and the van-driver, a villainously ugly little fat man with dark glasses and the worst set of teeth I had seen yet, even for a Sardinian, offered me a lift to Oristano. I dumped my rucksack and water-bag in with the gas-bottles and waited while the driver carried on a long and plaintive discourse with the motor-cyclist about some altercation he had had with someone who had hit the back of his van. Eventually they finished and we squeezed into the tiny cab, and took off with a deafening roar which mercifully precluded conversation: my meagre Italian had been exhausted that day.

The driver gripped the handlebars—these three-wheeled vans are primitive in the extreme—and we chugged, swaying and rocking, out of the Piana di Abbasanta into a cool green river valley. Covertly observing the driver, I noticed that without the dark glasses he was horribly cross-eyed. He wore a little blue greasy beret, and his regulation six-day stubble covered both of his chins. There was no provision in the cab for two passengers, so the journey was cramped, uncomfortable and hot, but when we had emerged from the river valley on to a dreary, bare, windswept coastal plain, the driver cut the engine and pulled up outside what at home would be described as a transport caff.

'The engine's too hot,' he said, 'we'll have to let it cool off. Coming in for a drink?'

The place was small, bare and functional. We pushed through half a dozen lorry drivers and before I could demur he had bought a quarter litre of red wine. He poured out two glassfuls, downed his in one gulp and left the rest to me. He then informed the assembled company that he had a captive maniac in the form of this Englishman, who was trying to walk through Sardinia. In point of fact I had so far been driven much further than I had walked, but as I had not asked for any of the lifts in essence I was still walking. The company smiled and shook its head. Why, it asked patiently, did I not travel by car, train or cycle? I couldn't explain properly, so remained, to them, a maniac. There was something to these Sards utterly incomprehensible about a man using his legs to get him about, when there existed easier and faster modes of travel. That, I later concluded, was the reason why people in the villages stared so: not because I was so obviously a stranger, a foreigner, but because I was equally obviously a wayfarer on foot by intent. In the British Isles I wouldn't rate a second glance, I would be commonplace; here, I was a twelve-foot Cyclops, with one eye in the middle of my face.

After we had resumed our journey, the driver, sweating considerably, stopped for a call of nature, and when he had finished suggested that I might pay for the next intake of petrol. Since we had done about thirty kilometres and the flimsy little vehicle was clearly never intended to carry a passenger, I thought this was reasonable. At the first Esso station in Oristano, after catching a far-off glimpse of the sea across the low, bleak coastal flats, we stopped and filled up (it only cost about nine shillings), shook hands and parted.

I went back to a convenient stretch of grass I had noticed where the road bridged the Tirso river; a flock of sheep and its shepherd were the only other occupants. While I was preparing dinner the shepherd strolled up for a chat. He was a young man, of twenty-three he said, but looked younger; he sprawled on the grass at my tent-flap, with his long shepherd's crook, rested his enormously thick forearms on the ground and asked me a series of questions that had my knowledge of Italian hard pressed and my pocket dictionary completely beaten. I told him the way I had come, south from Santa Teresa di Gallura.

'You've missed the best part of Sardinia,' he commented, 'why didn't you go through the Nuoro district? The mountains and forests there are much more beautiful than this western part.' The plain fact was that, after Corsica, I was fed up with climbing mountains, but I couldn't tell him that. I mention this to point out that although I have had to describe possibly the less interesting parts of Sardinia through my own indolence (I have already admitted to an idle nature) there do exist these more fascinating mountainous regions. If I ever go back to the island I shall take good care not to miss them again: through my omissions, perhaps other prospective visitors also will be guided there.

The young shepherd went at last and I finished my dinner. But visiting was not yet over for the night: just as my coffee was about to boil, there came a tremendous bleating, stamping and pushing as another flock of sheep surged under the bridge and all around me and I found I was at home to another shepherd. This one was an older man, of forty or so, as economical with razor blades as everybody else. He sat down for a chat in the same way as his predecessor, and after the preliminary questions we established that although he could speak Spanish he had never got around to French or English, which left us where we started. This, it seemed was because in 1937 he had volunteered to fight in the Spanish Civil War (he didn't say for which side). I told him about my plan to write about the three countries I was visiting.

'Yes,' he said, 'it is good to travel. I wish I could. Apart from Spain, I have only been for a short time to Italy. Travelling needs money, and I am a shepherd. There's no money in sheep, it's bad, very bad. But I often camp, like you, to be near my sheep. I'm doing that tonight, quite near, so we shall be neighbours.'

There are times when a sequence of minor irritations can annoy you more than one much worse catastrophe. The morning by the Tirso bridge was one of them. It started with the continuous racket of traffic on the road, but the road nuisances began while I was striking camp. First a thistle quill scored a double top in my thumb; this caused a delay while I got it out, and by that time a shower had come on, before I could get everything packed away. The last straw was when the zip on my rucksack split behind the fastener when I was doing it up.

I had calmed down a bit by the time I had passed the long row of petrol stations, minor shops and small houses and come into the Piazza Roma, the centre of Oristano. In the centre of the town stood the Torre di San Cristoforo, a fine tall bell-tower which lost some of its dignity when you saw it from behind because it was backless, like a stage set. I shopped for money, stores and postcards, and wandered round the town. The best part was at the far end from the Piazza Roma of a little passage way, rather reminiscent of Cecil Court, Charing Cross Road. Beyond it was a

TORRE S. CRISTOFORO,
ORISTANO

fine piazza between the most elegant classical buildings I had yet seen in Sardinia: in the centre, a statue of Eleonora of Arborea.

Arborea is the district of which Oristano is the principal town. When Sardinia had been under Byzantine domination, there had been a succession of elected Judicats, or judges, governing the island; when Byzantium abandoned the island the Judicats carried on, eventually becoming quite independent. Around A.D. 1000 the island was reckoned too big for control by one Judicat, so it was split into four districts, with a Judicat to rule each. They were elected from the most prominent of Sard families, and were obliged to take advice from an assembly of free citizens, who were more numerous than serfs. This remarkably democratic regime presided over Sardinia for all too short a time free from influence by any other power. In the late eleventh century the Pope, noticing that Sardinia was prosperous and therefore desirable, had the incredible effrontery to proclaim it Church property, and threaten invasion if it refused to acknowledge his sovereignty. The Judicats of the four districts made the classic mistake of bringing in foreign help against their enemy: they made an alliance with Pisa, which was competing fiercely with Genoa and Marseille for trade supremacy in the Western Mediterranean; the Pope backed Genoa and there was war.

It is the end of independence when strong outside powers start gaining control by such persuasive methods of pointing out what would happen if they didn't lend their force for defence. It's the age-old protection racket: throughout the twelfth and thirteenth centuries the Judicats allied themselves with Pisa and Genoa as circumstances decreed; they lost their independence, and the island lost its prosperity.

By the end of the fourteenth century three of the Judicats had succumbed and the Pope, despite strong resistance from the Judicat of Arborea, the only remaining Sard ruler with any real power, invested the King of Aragon as King of Sardinia.

Eleonora of Arborea was the last native-born Sard ruler. When she died, at the end of the fifteenth century, Sardinia lost its soul to foreigners. The Aragonese beat the Pisans and gained control of the island, which they very soon wrecked. They dispossessed the Sard landowners, enslaved the people, and split the land up between Spanish aristocrats. Taxation was worse even than under the Byzantines.

So Eleonora of Arborea is remembered in Oristano, and the last five hundred years are remembered in places like Mores, and Bonorva, and Macomer.

There are an amazing number of barber's shops in Sardinian towns, almost as many as there are bars. How they all manage to stay open is even more amazing, when you consider that the national emblem of the Sard appears to be a six-day stubble. I never came very close to solving this mystery, being permanently unshaven myself: I was more interested in seeing the country women in the Oristano streets, in long skirts and black shawls, setting up stalls to sell vegetable produce and pastries. When I was in Cagliari later on I noticed all the souvenir shops full of dolls in sundry traditional bright and decorative costumes: I never saw any of these, probably they only come out at festival times, but the stolid conservatism of the dress of these women, young and old, was the strangest thing to my eyes. Until, that is, I reached North Africa: the Muslims are the most conservative people in the world.

On my way out of town, to rejoin the main Cagliari road, I encountered a group of students. I said, 'Buon giorno.'

One said, 'Vous êtes français?'

'Non, je suis anglais.' Which delighted a small bespectacled lad at the back, who said, 'Speak English?'

'Yes, of course.'

'By Jove! Are you a tourist?'

'Not exactly.' I told him about my travels, and all the others (half a dozen or so, two of them girls) listened closely.

'By jove! And after Cagliari?'

'I'll get a boat to Tunis.'

'By Jove! And all these places will be in the book? By Jove! Good evening!'

I grinned and passed on—it was an hour or two before lunchtime!

Santa Giusta, the first village down the road, was the usual browbeaten sort of place, of low seedy cottages, much afflicted with poles and wires of every description, and of no artistic or pictorial merit whatsoever. Its church was another matter altogether. It had stood high above the village and the drab plain since the eleventh century, a mass of imperishable stone. How many successions of village dwellings the tall bell tower and high narrow nave have reared over in their thousand years' existence can only be imagined: the present collection do not look good for more than another generation or two. But what a fine, free, soaring building, this church! Inside, either side of the sky-high, coffin-narrow nave, a colonnade of round arches, a differently decorated capital to each column, lined the path to the altar like an avenue of old dark trees. Here, unlike the paint-and-plaster in the other churches I had visited, the walls had been left, bare stone; the only adornments in the usual elaborate style were in the saints' side chapels. The trace of incense, always present in Catholic churches, mingled with the musty smell of dead centuries, and the silence, protected from the road noise outside by thick stone walls, was itself a sound.

I sat peacefully meditating for a while, then the big door swung open and a coach-load of tourists, out from Cagliari so I noticed from the coach, began to trickle in with oohs and ahs and cameras everywhere. I rose, went out, picked up my rucksack from the terrace outside, and trotted down the steps back to the road. As I was leaving the village I was overtaken by a shower of rain and an urge to eat something, so I dived into an unfinished house and had lunch.

The main road, called Via Occidentale Sarda, now led straight across the Campidano Plain, an immense tract of land cutting right across the south-west of the island from Oristano to Cagliari. The landscape was unearthly flat, bleak, windswept, and, I must admit, tedious. Near Santa Giusta there was a red-fringed shallow lake called Stagno di Santa Giusta, a break in the scenery's monotony which reminded me of a Norfolk Broad. Here there were trees, mainly eucalyptus, lining the road, but out in the country there was nothing, just bare land up to the bordering hills, not even much cultivated; here and there were small farmsteads, where a man and horse struggled, ploughing, across a stony field. Mostly it was just grassland, with the wind whistling through it and the dark clouds looming up again in the west.

I had plodded along six or seven miles of this, meeting no one but a few boys with buckets full of mushrooms, waving them at passing motorists in the hope of inducing them to stop and buy, and the light was getting worse, the wind stronger and the clouds lower and darker. It was clearly going to pour down again, and if today's lift was going to materialise at all, it couldn't pick a better time or place.

Providence was still keeping an eye on me: just as the first monstrous raindrops came sloshing down, a car, modern and cream painted, stopped and the driver waved at me. I galloped over and got myself and kit stowed away inside it, and before the driver even had time to let in the clutch the rain was banging down, bouncing off the road, sweeping across the plain and saturating everything in sight. I breathed a thankful prayer and tried to concentrate on what the driver was saying. He was a plump young fellow of about my own age, jovial, and keen to show me the finer points of his car, which was new and his pride and joy. He was anxious to know what I thought of his fellow Sards, whether they were fine, generous fellows like himself, or stingy, miserable blackguards. I reassured him as best I could: in point of fact I had met nothing but courtesy, hospitality and amity throughout my journey.

We passed through the villages of Uras, full of horse-and donkey-cart traffic, Sardara and Sanluri, none of which gave me the impression that Sard house-builders had the edge on their Corsican equivalent. Soon after Sanluri, still in the middle of Campidano but nearer the hills, with the rain stopped and the weather brightening, we stopped at a crossroads.

'You can come with me to Siliqua, if you like, it isn't far from Cagliari.'

I explained that I didn't have to get to Cagliari until Sunday because that was when my ship was supposed to sail, so I would leave him here and see a bit more of the Campidano countryside in the meantime.

The only thing wrong with that plan was the weather: it rained, on and off, all next day. I had left the main road at the crossroads and camped half a kilometre from it on the way to Samassi. It was diabolical: great windswept acres of grass, sheep and artichokes; a shiny wet dead-straight road, full of whiskery characters driving horse-and-carts to market in, presumably, Sanluri, and the rain. Samassi was a large, sprawling, muddy, miserable place where the workless loiterers still loitered despite the rain and what shops there were cowered anonymously beneath a grimy overlay of mud and grey dinginess. All the houses were built of dreadful mud and straw bricks and seemed on the point of sliding slimily away across the road, down into the brown river. In fact the latter, the Mannu, was so littered with junk I think some of them already had.

But there was something of interest yet: along one section of the street, which was awash with a viscous solution of dung and mud, there were blank mud-brick walls, pierced now and then by huge, wooden, arched doorways. A wicket gate in one of these, swinging open, made me stop and stare: inside, behind this drab, sordid façade, there was a clean-swept cobbled yard, and a bright, neat little house with a verandah gay with tubbed, potted and climbing flowers. A peep through other open doors in this grey wall showed me the same kind of secret charm behind it.

Five wet kilometres after Samassi I came to Serramanna, which was just the same. I stopped in the first bar on the left for refreshment (a huge tumblerful of red wine for about sevenpence); it was a bare, dingy place, where in one room a crowd of lads were laughing and chatting over a meal and in the other a hideous old man with a glass eye and a thin grey face expressed contempt for a foreign traveller who knew so little Italian. The bar, over which this character presided, was tatty and paint-starved, the few chairs old and unsafe. This was Campidano, the most fertile part of the island.

STREET GATE IN SAMASSI

Serramanna had a large pantiled church, with many transepts, a dome and campanile in the square Byzantine style, and nothing much else of interest except some more of these intriguing court-yards behind concealing mud-brick walls. All these villages were so big, the drab houses seemed to drag on for ever, and when I came face to face with a crowd of schoolchildren, all in little lace collars with coloured bows, the girls in white smocks, the boys in black, I couldn't help reflecting that when they grew up there would hardly be one job to stretch between them all.

Through acres of artichokes and asparagus, cabbages and rain I came to Villasor, which should have been called Villasordid. The mixture was as before, the rain was relentless, and outside the village I was glad to accept a lift offered by a gentle-mannered monk in a brown habit and a full grey beard. His sandalled feet accelerated us along five miles or so of road to Decimomannu, where I gave up the uneven struggle with the elements and found a field of clover and thistles in which to huddle my damp and steaming person beneath my saturated tent.

The day I reached Cagliari was a Saturday and for a change

ORATORY OF S. GIOVANNI,
ASSEMINI

it was fine. The road was just as Campidano, dull as ever, but the villages were a little cleaner; outside Assemini there was a lovely little mediaeval chapel, the Oratory of San Giovanni, and in Elmas there was a domed bell-tower and a central garden place, set about with flower-beds and gaily coloured benches, from which to regard it. I lunched there in the sunshine, then decided to sketch the bell-tower; as soon as I put pencil to paper there appeared around me, as if by magic, a circle of children, in their white and black smocks, lace collars and silk bows. I am not sure their remarks were entirely complimentary.

The approaches to Cagliari were as ugly as those to any city,

and that is all I am saying about them. At long last I arrived at
the main thoroughfare of Cagliari, the Via Roma, that place of
shops and cafés and big hotels, colonnaded, arcaded and for ever
crowded, that runs along beside the waterfront.

I stayed in Cagliari for three days: I hadn't meant to stay more
than one, but it was Nice all over again, with me going to the
shipping office every day and being told no, there is no boat today,
it will leave tomorrow.

Cagliari is a town which rises on a hill and spills down it to the
water's edge. At the top is a mediaeval castle with a massive
keep, Torre dell'Elefante: I have no information about the de-
rivation of this name, I can only assume (probably erroneously)
that there is some connection with Carthaginian days, and Hannibal's elephants. Around the castle and towards the top of the
hill are the narrow, steeply sloping streets and tall tenement
houses of the old town; from them are cut wide, handsome
boulevards sloping down to the fashionable Via Roma at the
bottom. I saw a good deal of both boulevards and side streets
(aptly named—they are all on their sides) on my first afternoon in
the city, because I had great trouble finding a reasonable hotel.
By reasonable I don't mean one replete with the comforts of bath-
rooms, service and deep-pile carpets—I had to reject one like
that, as it was. It happened this way: I asked a policeman—one
of the city police, in flashy black and red, with white gloves—to
recommend a small inn or hotel. To add weight to my request I
was of course in my customary hobo outfit, and by that time very
tired because I had been plodding all over town, still rucksack-
laden, most of the afternoon. He directed me up one of the broad,
fine boulevards, lined with majestic grey buildings containing all
manner of doctors, solicitors and accountants, and right at the
top the small, inexpensive albergo turned out to be the brand
spanking new Hotel Jolly, a sort of minor Hilton. Slightly crazed
by this time I pushed through the glass swing doors, and sauntered across the lush carpet to the reception desk.

I felt, rather than saw, the attention of a dozen pairs of well-
dressed eyes. The chic, and very pretty, young lady at the reception desk kept magnificent control of her expression. I removed
my hat and smiled at her. 'Have you a room, please?'

My lady stared, uncomprehending. She swallowed, blinked,
and said 'I will see, sir. Would you like one with a bath?'

'No, no.' It would cost a fortune.

Much later, the possibility occurred to me that I may have been generating a deodorant-advert pungency that suggested to the dear girl my urgent need for one.

She called to a good-looking lad in porter's uniform and whispered to him. The porter looked me up and down, smiled amiably and asked for how long I wanted the room. By this time I was less

enthusiastic about taking it so I enquired after its cost. Doubtless my expression, on hearing it, told its own story, because the porter took me on one side and suggested gently that I tried a smaller, more suitable Pensione just up the road.

Of course I failed to locate this, but after eight more enquiries and three more recommendations I found a splendidly seedy place in the Via Sassari, almost exactly at the point where I had first entered the town.

Once I was able to relax, clean myself up, and walk out without being weighed down by my pack, I enjoyed Cagliari. Especially, I liked the Via Roma where everything seemed to happen, and the harbour. Boats appeal to me, I can wander around a fishing harbour for ages, just looking at the rhythmic curves of the boats, the rippling water, the unhurried activity of the fishermen mending and drying their nets, clearing up on board, paddling in dinghies from one craft to another, calling to each other, laughing, joking, arguing, smoking. The wharves, too, where the Tirrenia company's big white packets tied up and disgorged their passengers and cargoes, and a constant supply of larger and smaller merchant ships loaded and unloaded, all this had a magic fascination for me and kept me away from visiting churches and museums I should, as a tourist, have seen.

I did plenty of wandering the streets of the city, uphill and down: one time I was looking for a cinema which was showing an English film I had missed, another I visited every bookshop and stationer in the city trying in vain to buy a map of Tunisia (in one shop they didn't even know where Tunisia was) but I always finished up in the Via Roma, sitting at a table outside one of its arcade cafés. From there I could see all Cagliari going by: exquisitely coiffured young men in fashionable suits, walking arm in arm; a minority of young women (where do they hide all the pretty ones?); brown-corduroyed, stubble-chinned countrymen, and stout old ladies in long, full skirts, shawls, and skin like crumpled wash-leather; soldiers, sailors and airmen, slouching round-shouldered with their hands in their pockets, as unmilitary as Italians, mercifully, always have been; a tragic profusion of beggars, cripples, and idiots, approaching café-table drinkers, one hand eternally outstretched and an inaudible whisper at their lips. One night when I was drinking red wine at a Via Roma bar, a man in the street went mad, shouting and raving and falling about, and at once a circle of onlookers and helpers gathered. Soon the police arrived with an ambulance, and he was taken away. I don't know if there was something in the ultimate depression of life in Sardinia that tended to crack their reason, but there seemed to be a disproportionate number of people out of their senses, in Cagliari. The younger son of the people who ran my hotel, a boy of sixteen or so, did nothing but run spasmodically about the place, twisting a piece of string close in front of his face,

and pushing his nose about with his fingers. It was a sombre edging to a picture otherwise lively and colourful.

Another advantage of café-lounging in the Via Roma was that, without leaving your seat, you could watch the ships coming and going in the harbour: at night it was exciting, at sunset breathtaking. A ship, a moving mass of lights, gliding silently over the dark, gleaming water, towards the flashing mole-lights: beyond, the grey-mauve shapes of the mountains across the bay sharply outlined against the yellow western sky: wild ragged splashes of magenta, crimson and scarlet, flared up from violent clouds, reflecting in the black water like sequins on a velvet gown.

Business as usual in the Via Roma.

Spanish domination of Sardinia, after two and a half miserable centuries, ended with the War of the Spanish Succession. The House of Savoy took over from Aragon, but any improvement in the change was not clearly noticeable. The Italian language was made official (and everyone speaks it, after a fashion, today, except in Alghero, where a form of Catalan is said still to prevail, and the new King of Sardinia made certain improvements. But the next one dissipated them again, so they were back at the beginning.

The French Revolution stirred up common people all over Europe: in Sardinia it sparked off a revolt which was led, as if in a romantic fairy-story, by an aristocrat called Giovanni Maris Angioy, an exceptional gentleman who threw himself wholeheartedly into the cause of the poor: that is, the majority of Sardinia's population. In 1793 the French, sympathetically answering a call for help from the peasant rebels, sent a fleet to attack Cagliari harbour. Unfortunately it was beaten off.

But the movement had gained momentum. The cities of Cagliari and Sassari, at either end of the island, formed a joint Democratic Party, championing the rebels. In 1796 the villagers of Logudoro refused to pay their taxes and joined them. Then the all-conquering Napoleon shattered the Italians and it seemed that Sardinia would come into its own again.

However Napoleon was not interested in rebellious minorities in countries he had already conquered. When he had signed a treaty with the King of Sardinia, Victor-Amedee III, he took no further interest whatsoever in the poor Sards. They were left to the mercy of a punitive expedition directed by the Count of

Turin, who seems to have been the worst thing to happen to Sardinia since Tiberius Gracchus. There are no happy endings to any of the stories in Sardinian history.

The ship that plied between Cagliari and Tunis, the *Campidano*, was in port on the third morning. She was not one of the sleek white steamers I had watched every day leaving for Civitavecchia and Palermo, she was a small, rusty old hooker that looked like an illustration for a Conrad novel. She would sail, they said at the Tirrenia office, at midday. I went aboard at eleven, and they were only just beginning to unload ship then. The grim young steward in charge of the nine passengers—four other men and four women—pointed out with some perturbation that I was devoid of a vaccination certificate, necessary, he said, for landing in Tunis. I had of course forgotten all about that possibility, but another steward said not to worry, I would be vaccinated when we arrived.

The unloading went on all afternoon, but we were requested not to leave the ship. I stayed on deck, watching the crew at work: they would shout and rage at one another, shake fists and appear on the point of a violent quarrel over some minor disagreement, then within the next minute they were laughing and joking, all acrimony forgotten.

At half past five the sun began to set, painting gold-dust on the masts and yards of the ships, changing the gulls into rosy flamingos and the mountains into charcoal. The covers were on the hatches, the derricks lashed down; the pilot came aboard from his little launch, a tug strained on the *Campidano*'s stern, the engines throbbed and the propellors thrashed, and she got under way. Slowly the *Campidano* moved across the harbour, away from the string of lights along the Via Roma, from the grey mass of the Cagliari hillside, capped by the Elephant Tower, all shadowed in the sun's last orange glow.

She set a course for Africa, and put to sea.

PART THREE

TUNISIA

Chapter Eight

TUNIS TO BIZERTA

Tirrenia, the Italian steamship company named after the Tyrrhenian Sea, is good value for money. Passage from Bonifacio to
Santa Teresa, an hour's journey, cost six shillings and sixpence.
Cagliari to Tunis, including a bed, two good meals and an early
breakfast, came to about three pounds. Admittedly the *Campidano* was not quite in the same class as a P & O liner, or even a
cross-channel ferry-boat. She was old and slow, rolled like a horse,
and was just a little short on passenger comforts. There was nowhere really comfortable to sit down for instance, just a wooden
bench, and the backless forms in the canteen; and then there were
the lavatories. Continental w.c.'s are apt to be difficult under
normal, terra firma circumstances: in a heavy sea on board ship
they are tantamount to dicing with death. Also the floor of ours
was usually an inch or two under water.

There was no need for the early breakfast. When I went on
deck at 8.30—and nearly got blown off it—the coast of Africa
was in sight, but that rusty old tub needed another five hours'
steaming before she docked in Tunis harbour. As we approached
the coast, an elderly Tunisian, who was the only other passenger
beside myself to venture up on deck, showed me the landmarks as
they came into sight. The mountainous island of Zembra loomed
up on our port bow; then we came closer to the mainland and
picked out the tall blocks of flats and hotels on the hilly, reddish
coast. There was Gammarth Plage, the beach where Tunisians

go for weekend relaxation in the hot summer. La Marsa, and Sidi-bou-Saïd on its clifftop; the huge Hotel Amilcar, and the white villas and palm-gardens of Carthage, where we could dimly make out a mass of ancient stonework down by the water's edge, and plainly the huge absurd Cathedral of Saint Louis right on top of the hill of Byrsa. Then we chugged slowly towards La Goulette and the entrance to the ship-canal.

The closer approaches to Tunis are weird and difficult to understand at first. On either side of the ship there is a thin strip of land, with a road and railway along one, and then—more water. A great wide wilderness of water, stretching away to the dim hills. Tunis lies at the head of this huge shallow lake, just inshore: to turn it into a port, a deep channel and harbour had to be dredged, five miles long, all the way to the sea. It took the *Campidano* a good hour to make it, and I thought it was going on for ever. We were all peering out of portholes (it was raining, and windy, making a very unsuitable introduction to Africa) and I noticed some large whitish wading birds on the fringe of the right-hand lake.

'Those birds,' I said to another elderly Tunisian who, judging by the state of his chin had been in Sardinia too long, 'are they flamingoes?' I thought I detected a pinkish tinge to their feathers: if only the sun had been out. . . .

'No,' he said, 'they are only some kind of ducks, on the lake.' I didn't argue—it was his country and he ought to know, but they were very odd-looking ducks.

We docked at half past one, and it was still raining. We were courteously received by the harbour authorities, who presented us with forms to fill in stating exactly how much foreign currency we were bringing in, and the request to get it changed into good Tunisian dinars immediately. This was fine, except that the banks were closed until half past two and I was in urgent need of a meal, but I forgot about this situation when I left the dockyard gates behind, picked my way through a loitering crowd of dockyard Arabs dressed mostly in faded blue dungarees and headgear loosely adapted from old towels, and made for the city.

I arrived soon at the bottom end of the Avenue Habib Bourguiba, near the terminus of the electric trains which run along the bank of the ship-channel to La Goulette and beyond. The Avenue Habib Bourguiba used to be called Avenue Jules Ferry, but since

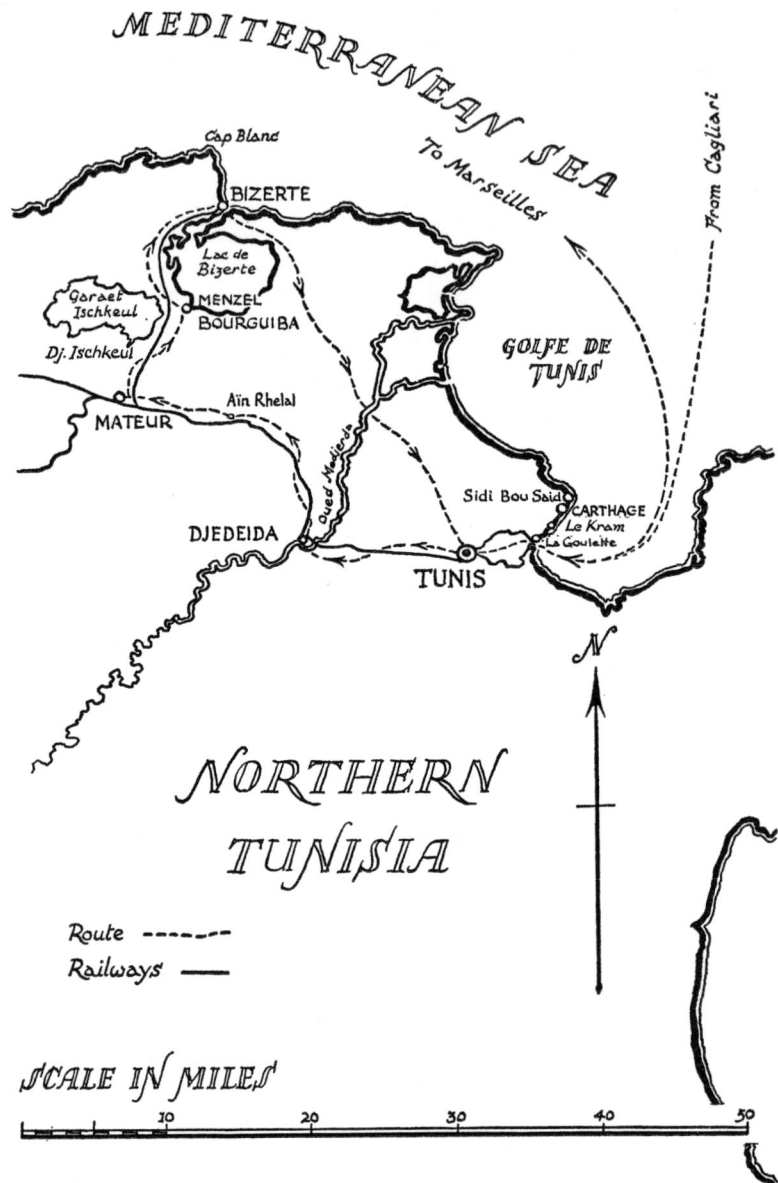

MEDITERRANEAN SEA

To Marseilles

From Cagliari

Cap Blanc

BIZERTE

Lac de
Bizerte

Garaet
Ischkeul

MENZEL
BOURGUIBA

Dj. Ischkeul

GOLFE DE
TUNIS

Aïn Rhelal

MATEUR

Oued Medjerda

Sidi Bou Said

CARTHAGE
Le Kram
La Goulette

DJEDEIDA

TUNIS

NORTHERN

TUNISIA

N

Route -------
Railways ———

SCALE IN MILES

| 10 | 20 | 30 | 40 | 50 |

the latter gentleman, when Prime Minister of France, was chiefly responsible for Tunisia becoming a French Protectorate in 1881, the erasion for his name in favour of the president of modern independent Tunisa, for the principal thoroughfare in Tunis, is understandable.

I found a decent, but not too extravagant-looking restaurant and walked in. I dumped my rucksack on the floor and removed my hat and simultaneously realised that I hadn't any Tunisian money. A waiter, a young man of negroid appearance, came up and I explained my predicament. A minute later I was explaining it again, to the manager.

'Oh, that's all right,' said he imperturbably, 'have your meal, and by that time the banks will be open and you can come back here and pay your bill.'

Beyond a vague idea that the dinar was a fairly large unit of currency, I was quite ignorant of the rate of exchange, so that when I saw the menu and every dish was priced in hundreds of something, I was apprehensive. Oh well, I thought, a good appetite like this shouldn't be wasted, so I ordered three courses and a half litre of wine and enjoyed it, and the bill came to seven hundred whatever-they-weres. When I reached the bank and started to learn about Tunisian pecuniary arrangements, I was surprised to find this was only about ten shillings.

The dinar is worth fourteen shillings or thereabouts, and it is subdivided into a thousand millims, which are the same value as the old French franc. A hundred millims are therefore worth one and fivepence.

Ignorance leads invariably to making mistakes: had I known about cheap hotels in Tunis, I would never have bothered looking for one, better run than the rest, because I eventually discovered that it does not exist. I had to learn by experience—and did! The waiter at the restaurant had recommended the Youth Hostel, but his directions were vague and I failed to locate it. There were several small hotels about, with imposing names like Hotel Regina and Hotel Royal, so I tried one. I asked, as usual, for a single room; I was shown a room in which were sitting, amid an incredible litter of rags, tatters and old rubbish, two Arabs. They both smiled politely at me, but I did not feel inclined to join them. In the next place I got no further than the reception desk, where a large grim-faced negro told me he had no single rooms,

would I share with others? I would not. The third was an establishment I afterwards christened Hotel des Souris, for reasons
which may already be obvious. It had a single room available,
and it was absurdly cheap, and I was prepared to overlook its
shabbiness because I was tired of trudging around town with my
rucksack. It was only after I had elected to stay in it that I started
wondering absent-mindedly why the walls were tiled instead of
painted or papered, and then realised that it had once been a
bathroom!

Having had no experience whatever of Tunisians, or Arabs of
any descriptions, I had no idea what they were like. So to be on
the safe side, I locked my door every time I left the room, no
matter how briefly. The first time I did this was just to visit the
lavatory, on the same corridor and as if impelled by some super-
natural force, at once I dropped my key down the pan. But the
most surprising phenomenon of that interesting house mani-
fested itself late that night.

I had passed the evening wandering about in the Avenue Habib
Bourguiba—the hotel was near the Porte de France, an ancient
gateway on the threshold of the old part of the city—and its
environments, locating the Post Office, and the best bars and
restaurants. I bought a map, collected some letters, and went to
dinner. In the restaurant I chose for this meal there were three
Americans, who were apparently working in Tunis: they were
representative of quite a number of their countrymen in the same
status. They were dining with a Tunisian, but carried on a loud
conversation in their own language, which he obviously had difficulty in following. This breach of courtesy apart, they made
coarse jokes, giggled like schoolboys, and gave a display of in-
civility unparalleled by the rudest of rural peasantry that I'd met
in the course of my travels. I was not impressed.

Escaping quickly I went to a bar crowded with people of all
shapes and colours from European white to darkest negroid black,
and in the most astonishing range of clothing. There were men
in modern tailored suits, some in traditional Arab robes, bare
legs and sandals, and quite a number in a mixture of the two.
Nearly everyone sported a little raspberry-red skull-cap, and the
most popular garment was a thick cloak with wide sleeves,
closed down the front, mid-calf length, with a huge hood. These
robes, in a variety of colours from black to a striped brown and

white, were patterned and tasselled in a set form: they seemed to
be a national garment. Women, who never ventured into the bars,
pattered past in the streets, peering out of their all-enveloping
white silk, silent. Shoeshine boys, one after another, wandered
round the tables with their boxes and brushes, touting for trade.
My boots were by this time in a dreadful state and past redemp-
tion, so I declined all offers. Then there were newspaper sellers,
peanut sellers, flower sellers, pastry sellers; everyone was busy trying to sell something, and how, at that time of year (it was now
late November) any of them made enough to keep alive, I don't
know.

The Arabs, I thought, were still an unknown quantity: they
all looked so basically grimy.

My hotel room, after I had retired to bed (the sheets were
reasonably clean but torn) very patently smelled of dampness. I
was just resigning myself to this and beginning to doze off, when
I was joined by the hotel mouse. This character, clearly not
worried by the damp, had run along the underside of my bed,
across the pillow six inches from my startled eyes, up the table leg
and into my rucksack foraging for food, before you could say
Habib Bourguiba. I had my torch handy, and shone it at the
rucksack, but the mouse was well down inside it and looked
like staying there. I left him at it, turned over and went to
sleep.

I was quite glad to leave the hotel, in the morning. I met the
owner in the hall when I was settling up, and he was so affable I
hadn't the heart to complain. This was just as well, because I discovered later that I had inadvertently taken away something
belonging to him.

The dockyard officials, while not unduly perturbed at my dis-
closure that I had no smallpox vaccination certificate, had mentioned that perhaps I ought to get one, because there was the
off-chance that I might not be allowed out of the country without
it. I could get inoculated, they said, with no trouble and less ex-
pense, at the Service d'Hygène, near the Marché Central. So first
thing after breakfast, which was coffee and croissants in a café
near the Porte de France, I went in search of it, and after going
all the way round the market, a huge covered place full of fruit,
vegetables and jostling early-morning Tunisians, and enquiring
half-a-dozen times, eventually asked a man for directions while

standing right outside its front door. In extenuation, there was nothing to indicate what it was. There was a row of men sitting in the waiting room and I thought it would take hours, but as soon as I had put my pack down someone asked what I wanted and I was in, jabbed, and out clutching my certificate before I knew what had happened. None of the waiters seemed to mind, in fact they all grinned and chaffed me amicably as I left.

It was a grand morning, and nothing except the mouse had happened during the night, and the sunshine and blue sky quickly turned Tunis into an experience to be enjoyed. I stocked up with provisions, chatted with the chap in the grocery, flirted with the girl in the bakery, had another coffee, then hit the road out of town. This led round the outside of the Medina, the ancient Arab part of the city, past multitudinous tiny shops, in groups of the same kind; a row of fruiterers would follow a row of pastrycooks, then a cacophonous, blue-sparking clanging iron-working section, and then a succession of cave-like barber's shops, at least half a dozen of them all crammed together, and all fully occupied. People thronged the pavements, in their picturesque variety of dress. I very much admired their thick hooded cloaks, and began to imagine myself in one. This journey through the tradesmen's entrance of Tunis, in the benevolent sunshine, did me a great deal of good, because I began to feel at home in the place, and to be less uncertain about the Arabs. When greeted with a bonjour or salud they all responded with a smile or a lift of the hand or both, and I noticed that the streets and houses were far cleaner than I had expected. Even the suburban road, outside the city limits, was interesting, because the houses were brilliantly white and designed in the old Moorish pattern, and still there were the people in their curious assortment of dress; the men in the ubiquitous red cap, the women so veiled and shrouded in white you could only just tell they were women. It was just as I was passing by the gate of a Tunisian Army barracks, where a slovenly soldier stood leaning on his rifle, that I met the first Englishman since I left home and the first fellow-tramp ever.

Roy Lewis, having caught up with me, accompanied me for the next four or five miles. He was from Birmingham, by way of Copenhagen, where he and a friend had washed dishes for three months; most of Europe including Spain; Morocco, Algiers and now Tunis. He had planned to go to Cairo and had sent money there, but was now completely broke and trying to get the money sent from Cairo to Tunis. The Tunis Youth Hostel having temporarily closed, he was on his way to the one at La Manouba, if he could find it. He had done most of it by hitch-hiking, for no reason other than boredom and frustration in a dull office job at home and the crying need for adventure.

We passed the great white palace of the Beys of Tunis, now the National Museum, at Le Bardo, all set about with palm trees and orange orchards. The road led straight into a wide, highly cultivated plain, where oranges, olives and vineyards abounded. After enquiring a couple of times we found what we thought might be the La Manouba Youth Hostel, and parted with mutual wishes for the best of British luck.

When, on the broad grassy strip beside the road, I stopped for lunch, I was immediately surrounded by a crowd of inquisitive men and children who appeared as if from nowhere. They were all very friendly, and when I had explained my presence, in French, to their spokesman, and he had relayed it in Arabic to the rest, they all shook hands with me, smiled, waved, and went to their homes. Then just as I was preparing to get back on the road, three little black children rolled up. I said hullo to them, and they grinned shyly, said hardly a word, then gave me two oranges, one already half-peeled.

I was beginning to have a great liking for Tunisians.

The country looked good: cleanly, prosperously cultivated to the limit, and irrigated by an extensive system of concrete conduits and channels. Orange orchards and vineyards, acres of grain crops and rows of market garden stuff unrolled on either side of the wide, straight road. In the distance there were hills, old and eroded, and crossed with parallel horizontal lines: they would be terraces. I passed through a couple of small villages, where people sat and lounged outside the shops and garages, in the sunshine, and greeted me with charm and courtesy. At once I was stopped by a crowd of young fellows, gathered by a petrol station. They questioned me closely, particularly wanting to know 'why are you on foot?' They seemed to be satisfied with my explanation, and I thought it would be a good time to hand out my usual compliments—which may be diplomatic but are also genuine—about how good the place looked, how rich the fields and how cheerful the people. This went down very well.

'Ah yes,' said one, seriously, 'but we have our President Bourguiba to thank for that.' This surprised me, because I have asked
Frenchmen about President de Gaulle and been assured that he
is the nearest thing to national disaster since Sedan, and you can
talk to Englishmen of either party and never hear anything to the
government's credit.

'He's a good man, is he?'

'Oh, yes. In our seven years of independence he has done a
tremendous amount to increase our prosperity.'

Well, good for him, and good for this young Arab for appreci-
ating him.

Quite soon after this, I met a handsome young chap on a
bicycle, with a wooden box balanced across his handlebars. We
started chatting, he cycling slowly along beside me for a distance,
and he told me he was an inspector for the Tunisian equivalent of
the Milk Marketing Board, and the wooden box contained milk
samples. He confirmed what I had observed, that the soil of this
northern region of the country was rich and productive.

We approached the town of Djedeida and my friend, whose
name was Youssef, told me that it, like most Tunisian towns, was
in two parts. One was the old, Arab town, with an ancient
mosque, small primitive houses and clay streets; the other, built
since France began to dominate the land, had metalled roads and
European-built, if Arab-styled, houses, including railway station,
Post Office and perhaps a bar or two. Youssef went home to
Tebourba and I crossed the meandering, muddy Oued Medjerda,
past the clustered dirty-white hutches and tall mosque tower
of the Arab town. On the banks of the river I was astonished to find a mass of new, modern buildings from which were
emanating the unfamiliar and incomprehensible notes of Arab
music. It was Radio City, the wireless and television centre. The
modern part of Djedeida contained just as many Arabs and
almost as many unsophisticated dwellings, clustered around the
railway station, as the old part. I found a bar, well patronised by
customers inside and out, sitting at tables in the sunshine and
swatting flies—I then made a *faux pas*. I had forgotten that
Arabs, as Muslims, are supposed to be teetotal.

'I'd like a beer, please.'

'No beer, monsieur.'

'Well, wine then.'

'Sorry, monsieur, we have no spirits or alcohol here. Only coffee, fruit juices, or Coca-Cola.'

I took my coffee to an outside table and joined the fly-swatters. It was good coffee, and amazingly cheap, considering that in France you can be charged three times as much for a tiny little cupful, and then it's usually tepid. If the Arabs can do it so cheaply, why can't the French?

The camp-site-finding problem in this part of Tunisia was the exact opposite to Corsica. There, the whole place was free as air, if you could find a square inch that wasn't on a ridiculous slope; here, it was flat as a football pitch, if you could find a square inch that wasn't growing something! Having acquired water from the bar, I eventually settled for a patch at the edge of a clover field. It wasn't very private, and while I was putting up my tent, settling in, preparing, cooking and eating my dinner I had a constant audience of six or seven onlookers, who seemed unable to tear themselves away from this unusual sight.

It was not one of my quieter nights in camp. Later in the evening, when it was dark, a couple of chaps turned up with a portable radio, and insisted on trying to find an English station for me. We heard a disjointed assortment of music, a barrage of atmospherics, and the results of two European Cup matches, one of which involved West Ham United. My last candle burned out. In the next field, ever since I had moved in, there had been a man on a tractor, driving round and round with a harrow. I fully expected him to stop when darkness fell, but he carried on, with headlights. Oh well, I thought, he'll stop before long, at eight perhaps.

He was still there, driving round and round that miserable field, at half past one in the morning, and when he did at last stop, the dogs took over!

At four a.m. came the *pièce de résistance*. I had been dozing, and was woken by a scrabbling sound. A bird, walking on the tent roof, I thought. There it was again, and something dropped, plop, onto my sleeping-bag-encased legs. I sat up and grabbed my torch.

Between my rucksack and the sleeping bag there lay a piece of bread which I had been saving for breakfast. Lumps had been nibbled out of it. The side wall of the tent had been pushed up, the groundsheet had been pushed down: through the hole between the two had escaped the Hotel Mouse, and he had tried to take my breakfast with him. He had been stowed away somewhere in my rucksack, the whole of that day.

I hope he made it back to the hotel: I should hate the owner to think I had stolen him.

The morning began late for me, but it was not far to Chaouat, the next village. In it were a large and splendid onion-spired twin-towered mosque, a decrepit Christian church, a huddle of dreary little one-storey cottages and three shops. It was not until the third shop, after I had strained my vocabulary to bursting point, that I discovered that in these parts, candles were not called chandelles, but bougies: probably all three shops had stocked them.

Chaouat was on the edge of the great plain, and after it the hills were closer: bare, wild, sweeping slopes that offered no hope either for agriculture or shelter. Near the village there stood on one of these open hillsides a collection of crude, primitive huts, made of mud and thatched with straw. On top of the hill there was a tiny white domed building, like one of the Corsican family mausoleums. Below the huts, nearer the road, there stood one of the famous old black tents of the Bedouin Arabs. Around these archaic dwellings wandered robed, tattered figures; donkeys, cattle and horses grazed the short grass, chicken scratched about in the heaps of rubbish and old muck that lay outside each habitation, children yelled and chased each other and women gossiped in doorways. Across the road from this cluster of semi-permanent nomadic dwellings there was a well, and there was a little scene at the well that made me think of illustrations for the Bible. Two women and a girl, having drawn water, were passing the time of day; their dresses were those of their ancestors, and so were the receptacles of the water. Tied to the back of a donkey, which the girl held still, were two slim, beautifully curved pitchers, with a handle each side. Another stood on the ground at the feet of one of the women. The woman of Samaria must have used just such a pitcher when she went to draw water from Jacob's Well at Sychar.

This countryside, so wide open and unsheltered, yet so diligently farmed, was the home of a surprisingly large number of people. There were several villages of these mud huts, and each one was bursting with inhabitants. Near Sidi Athman, distinguished from its squalid fellows by a crossroads and a railway station (the railway had followed the road all the way from Djedeida), a man going home to lunch from his work in the fields, cycled over to me and stopped. He hadn't much French (I had already discovered that conversation with most of the country people was limited to bonjour, ça va, and au revoir) but he was completely at a loss, like the Sardinians, to understand why I was on foot, and since he couldn't understand when I told him, he stayed mystified. He kept pointing to the railway, and saying 'train, train,' which I found slightly irritating.

The approaches to the first gradient since leaving Tunis were ornamented by the splendidly substantial whitewashed buildings, set on a verdant hillside, of the Domaine Sakkuk, whose vineyards marched out across the land, whose fields flamed a vivid Provençal orange, whose olive and orange orchards striped the hills in regimental ranks; whose owner (a Tunisian Arab by his name on the notice board) obviously knew a thing or two about farming for profit. This was the kind of place originally set up, probably, by a French colonist, the kind of place they said would fall to rack and ruin as soon as the Arabs had it to themselves.

At the top of the gradient was a turgid village called Aïn Rhelal, mostly mud-huts, ragged Arabs, goats, dogs and moth-eaten donkeys, and I had the misfortune to fall in with a character in a tattered brown cloak who turned out to be the village idiot. He accompanied me all the way through the various parts of the village, which were scattered, and kept asking questions. I wouldn't have minded that, of course, but when I answered a question which I thought was in French, and he asked it again and again and wouldn't answer mine, I realised he didn't know a word of French but it didn't stop him asking questions. We passed the railway station and shortly afterwards found a convenient grass plot by the roadside. It was a bit public, but so would anything else have been: there was hardly a tree in sight and the only bushes were occasional clumps of prickly pear. Horace was still with me by the time I had installed myself in my tent, and he sat down at the tent-flap as if he meant to stay the night. We had a somewhat profitless and sterile discussion, but from his gestures I divined that he wanted something to eat, drink and smoke. I hadn't too much myself, but I gave him some water and bread, but as I don't smoke, couldn't oblige with a cigarette. He didn't believe me, and kept chattering away in

Arabic, asking the same questions over and over again, until I got rather fed up with him.

'Look, you silly-born twerp,' I mentioned, in English, 'it's no good you going on like this because I haven't the slightest idea what you're talking about. Why don't you go home?'

Eventually, nothing more by way of victuals being forthcoming, he gave up and went. I watched him wander aimlessly up the bare grassy hill towards the mud-huts at the top, breathed a thankful prayer, and started to get my dinner. Five minutes later a lad in a straw boater, of all things, rode slowly up on a bicycle, stopped, and stared, then came over to my tent. 'Oh no, not another one.' Horace had stayed an hour, as it was, and soon it would be quite dark.

But young Gilani ben Khemaïs Riahi was a different proposition altogether. His thin dark face was full of intelligence, he spoke excellent French, and he spoke sensibly and agreeably. He chatted while I had my dinner and washed up, telling me that he lived with his parents in the railway station (his father was foreman of track-repairers). Noticing that I was now perilously short of water, he very nobly offered to take my water-bag home, and come with it, filled, after his dinner.

It had been dark for a long time when he returned. He approached me sheepishly, hobbling, wheeling his bike.

'I'm terribly sorry,' he said, 'I fell off my bike in the dark. I've hurt my foot—and I've holed your bag!'

He held it out for me to see: it was spurting like a fountain pen from a three-cornered hole where it most mattered. I assured him that it didn't matter in the slightest (it was catastrophic) that I could easily mend it (impossible) and that I certainly would not have to buy a new one, but thank you very much for offering to pay for it. (I certainly would have to buy a new one.) I patched up a nasty gash on his leg, and once reassured that I was not in a towering, frenzied rage, he sat down and prepared to give me the most valuable collection of information I had so far heard in Tunisia.

Gilani was nineteen or twenty years old, and had qualified by apprenticeship as a solderer: he now worked in a metal-working shop in Menzel Bourguiba. 'Ask me,' he said, 'anything you like about Tunisia. If I know the answer, I'll be glad to tell you.'

'Well, to start with, what's the name of that thick robe, with a hood, that nearly everyone seems to wear?'

'That's the cachabiya.'

'Is it peculiar to Tunisia?'

'Not really. Only in Algeria they call it a djellaba.'

'What's a djebba, then?'

'That's a summer dress. It's long and flowing, and made of much finer material, and if you are rich enough you can have it patterned with gold, and designs in coloured silk.'

'I notice that everyone also wears a little red cap. What's that called?'

'The chechiya.'

'And the women are always in white.'

'Yes, but they only wear the white robe, called ha'ik, when they are going somewhere, out in public. It is the custom. Sometimes they also wear a veil, called lahfa. But not so many, nowadays. At home they wear their ordinary clothes, in whatever colours they please.'

'Yes, I saw a couple at a well today, unveiled and in blue or black or something. Oh, and you know those big earthenware pitchers they get the water in? What do you call them?' I drew the outline of the long, slender amphora that had put me in mind of the woman of Samaria.

'That's a gargolette.'

'These women were loading their gargolettes on to a donkey. There are plenty of donkeys round here, but I thought you used camels for transport in North Africa. I haven't seen a camel yet.'

'You won't, either, in this part of Tunisia. You have to go down south to the desert country, they use them there all right. Even then, camels are more commonly used in Libya than in Tunisia. It's donkeys and horses here, all the time. You're going to Mateur tomorrow?'

'Yes. About fifteen kilometres, isn't it?'

'About that. Mateur's the biggest market in Northern Tunisia for donkeys and horses. On Fridays it's open for the sale of brebis, that's female donkeys; on Saturdays, it's male donkeys, horses and cattle. If you get there early enough you'll see the market, tomorrow being Saturday. It's quite interesting.'

'I bet it is.' I produced my map and showed it to him. 'Look, here's Mateur. I want to go on from there to Bizerta: what's the country like between the two?'

'Oh, very beautiful. You see this lake, on the left of the road? Well the hilly country round that is the wildest in the North. That hill's Djebel Ischkeul. There are all kinds of wild animals there, wild boars, foxes, jackals, deer, lions—'

'Lions?'

'Certainly. It's very wild country.' Maybe, but lions? 'If you are camping there,' Gilani went on, 'you should take care, because the animals are extremely fierce.' He's pulling my leg—must be. Lions? Change the subject.

'I'm surprised to see so many of those awful mud huts in the villages. They look terribly primitive.'

FARM NEAR MATEUR

'The gourbis? Yes, they are. But so many of the people here are still very poor, you know. My father is not at all well off, and he's got a good job and we live in the railway station, so you can see what it's like for these other people.'

Gilani and I chatted on, in the candlelight at the opening to my tent, for a while longer, before he stood up and decided to go home. 'I'll come and see you off in the morning,' he said.

He did, too. He stood and watched me pack up, and then extorted a promise to correspond with him when I returned home; he shook hands with great emotion and waved me out of sight down the road to Mateur.

Well now I knew an Arab in his cachabiya and chechiya riding his brebi, loaded with gargolettes, towards his gourbi, when I saw one. Learn the right jargon and you're half way towards getting the feel of the country.

It was a beautiful sunny morning, with a light breeze, like a spring day in England. From the top of one of the mild hills I could see Mateur, a white splash on a hilltop, about five miles away. Beyond it, across the fertile brown-soiled plain, there were mountains, the range along the sea-coast west of Bizerta. Several gourbi mud-hut villages splattered untidily about the wayside, but farms looked prosperous; there was one just off the tree-shaded approach-road to Mateur that I admired particularly, a place of fine strong buildings where a wind-pump whirred in the breeze above white walls, palm trees and prickly-pear hedges. The road was filled with a constant procession of cattle, horses, mules and asses, accompanied by men, children and wheeled carts, from Mateur market.

Mateur was an Arab town: I didn't see a single European there. Architecturally it was plain, a close-packed mass of cubic one-storey hutches, but whitewash and sky-blue woodwork allevi-ated what would otherwise have appeared squalid. The cattle and horse market was over, but the place was still seething with people; from the railway station up to the town a succession of taxis plied to and fro, jingling, clattering two-horse carriages carrying white-shrouded women and eccentrically dressed men. Although I rated plenty of stares, I felt less outlandish than usual, because the variety of dress among everyone else was so aston-ishing. I rested outside a bustling café and drank coffee (at three-pence a glass) and unobtrusively studied my company.

The traditional chechiya was the standard headgear, often the basis for a sort of turban, a length of cotton or towelling wound round the head and twisted into a knot at one side. Below that anything went: for some the cachabiya, with bare legs and sandals, was *de rigueur*; for others, a ghastly ragged blanket or sheet, wrapped and folded and draped; but most were in a baffling assortment of European dress, military in flavour. Baf-fling, that is, until I saw the second-hand clothes shop across the way that was selling bits of surplus uniforms from every army in Europe and a couple in America. Passers-by were numerous and heterogeneous—I never knew before there were so many shades of brown—and mostly male, although I did notice one or two eye-catching young ladies swathed seductively in their white silk, giving nothing away but flashing glances from dark eyes and the general impression, conveyed in their graceful step, that beneath their voluminous, cunningly folded ha'iks was concealed volup-tuous femininity.

Suddenly voices were raised above the general babble—a violent altercation was raging between a café customer and one of the shoe-shine boys who, as in Tunis, made a damned nuisance of themselves by continually touting for custom. This one, who couldn't have been more than twelve years old, eventually departed in tears and in a flaming temper.

Gilani's accident with my water-bag having made the purchase of a new one a necessity I wandered round the crowded market streets looking for plastic water-bottles. There were plenty of shops, and plenty of 'we haven't got one but Yakub here will show you a shop that might' but no one had anything like a plastic bottle. I could have bought a very fine light aluminium can, but my mind at that moment chose to stop functioning properly, which it does at times, and I thought confusedly that three hundred millims were three thousand, which would be absurdly expensive for a water-can. The shop-keeper was much too polite to say so, but he must have thought me extremely mean when I told him three hundred was too dear. Under five shillings what did I expect, miracles? It was not until I had been directed from shop to shop by an obliging group of small boys and actually bought a plastic can in the same style as the metal ones but at a higher price, that I realised my mental aberration. I felt very stupid, and kicked myself all the way out of Mateur.

On one side of my roadside camp that evening loomed the dark mass of Djebel Ischkeul; on the other, a wild flaring African sunset blazed across the windy sky. In between was a small gourbi village with more howling, whining, shrieking dogs, it seemed, than people.

The Bizerta road cut like an arrow across the moon-like landscape; great flat windswept fields of winter wheat lay on either side, and the only trees in sight were the ones lining the road. Even they were absent after a while. Traffic was infrequent, but it included one man who stayed with me for two or three miles. Taking the trouble to dismount from his bicycle and approach me to satisfy his curiosity (what nationality was I and why was I on foot) he seemed eager to continue the conversation, so I encouraged him. He was about forty, a stockily built man in European-type working clothes, bare-headed, with a swarthy face and little black moustache.

'You people,' I said, waving at the vast square miles of growing wheat, 'have certainly got this place well cultivated.'

He liked that, as I thought he would. 'Yes,' he said, 'but you
should have seen it when the French were here. Like a desert. No
progress at all. They wouldn't spend money on us, see? You see
that school over there—' (a dreadful place to put a school—apart
from a couple of gourbi villages there was nothing else in sight)
'—and the one back in Mateur? All built since the French went.
President Bourguiba started loaning money for improvements
like that. We owe a lot to him. Before, it was a misery. Now,
Tunisia is a good place to be in.' His command of the French
language, whether the old colonists had bothered to educate him
or not, was pretty good.

'More work for everybody, I suppose, and not so much unem-
ployment?' I suggested.

'Not much. We're not rich, mind, by a long way, but most of
us have at least got enough for our daily bread. We're much
better off than Algeria.'

'How so?'

'Well, since Independence we've got our own dignity back.
Everyone mixes in together, there's no prejudice against class,
colour, race or religion. In Algeria there are still a lot of the old
French families, and they treat the Arabs as inferiors. Here we're
all Tunisians, and proud of it.'

'I see.' Even with a pinch of salt to season the man's enthusiasm, if he could be taken as a fair representative of the working
Tunisians then the new Republic and its president would seem to
be popular in that quarter if not in others. He went on heatedly
about the French preference for serving their own interests first
and those of Tunisians second, of taking much out of the country
and putting little back in, in the time-honoured habit of colonists.
We passed by a group of derelict wooden huts, close by a level
crossing of the railway.

'That was an army camp, before.' He meant before Tunisia's
independence, but I was finding out that it was unnecessary, in
conversation, to refer to that painful era by any more elaborate
term than 'Avant'.

'I suppose a lot of you were in the French Army during the
war?'

'Oh, yes, many. I was myself.' That did it. He went off into a

lengthy chronicle of his martial activities and became rather excited and incoherent when he reached the bit where (if I understood him correctly) he had wiped out two German machine-gun
posts with a single hand-grenade. 'But it didn't do me any good,'
he said sadly, wiping the spittle of his narrative from his chin, 'I
was just as poor at the end of the war as I was at the start.'

We climbed a low hill and overlooked a wide, shallow, mud-
coloured lake rimmed with the Djebel Ischkeul mountains. Here,
according to Gilani, be dragons. I asked my new friend about the
lions, but he was vague. The lake, anyway, was packed with
fish, he said, but catching them was prohibited. I was sure that
didn't stop some of the local people, on dark nights.

We pushed on towards Menzel Bourguiba for a while, chatting
inconsequentially, then observing regretfully the passage of time,
my companion mounted his bicycle and departed. I could see
the white houses of Menzel Bourguiba, and those of its neigh-
bouring village Tindja, and beyond them a flash of water, a
deeper marine blue than the previous lake. That would be the
Lake of Bizerta, just inland from the sea, reputedly one of the
finest natural harbours in the Mediterranean.

Fairly obviously, Menzel Bourguiba is a new name for the
town. It was changed for the same reason as the name of the
widest street in Tunis: it used to be named after Jules Ferry. As
Ferryville it was an important naval dockyard, but the departure
of the French, navy and all, meant that to prevent Menzel Bourguiba from declining into an apology for its fine new name, an
alternative industry had to be established. From the low hills
above the town I could see the shapes, glinting in the sun, of some
weird functional structures down by the lakeside: whatever it was,
that project was already under way.

From the direction I approached it, Menzel Bourguiba looked
just as archaic as Mateur. People of both sexes and all ages, on
foot and mounted on bicycle or donkey, thronged the road,
coming provision-laden from the town to the rows of tiny white-
walled, flat-roofed houses which had replaced the gourbis. I've
seen more palatial pig pens, but compared with the gourbis they
were Paradise. The first part of the town proper was a wide open
space near the railway station where a market similar to that of
Mateur was still in progress. On all sides were little shops,
stalls, and dealers with horses, mules, donkeys, chicken, ducks

and turkeys, all of which livestock was whole-heartedly contributing to the general clamour, which was deafening. Feeling in dire need of revival I called at the first bar I could find, sat at one of the shabby old tables outside, and had two quick coffees. These were brought out with all due ceremony and the customary glass

MENZEL BOURGUIBA

of water (presumably as a chaser) by a skeletal old scarecrow in a ragged approximation to a turban and the indescribably tattered remains of a white overall.

Feeling better, I crossed the railway line and presently arrived at a minor sort of étoile, radiating wide streets, lined with imposing white buildings and full of palm trees, flowerbeds, and an enormous statue of the President. Among the buildings were the

Post Office and the Town Hall, and both of these were in the traditional Moorish design, intricately decorated, and immaculate in fresh whitewash and sky-blue paintwork. Taking one of the fine streets I came soon to a park-like square, the Place de la République, with a bandstand in its middle and more Moorish architecture all around. Overcome by the discovery of the first real bar since Tunis, with tables and chairs on the pavement à la Française, I occupied one and ordered a beer. When this came, I thought for a moment I'd made a mistake and ordered a meal, because with it, entirely without charge, were served dishes containing apricots and olives (for increasing the thirst) and briques au poisson. Briques are a Tunisian speciality, a square of crisp batter folded over whatever you care to have inside: I will treat later of the difficulties of brique à l'oeuf.

The waiter was still laying out the last dish of this collation when a large gentleman rolled up and started asking him in a mixture of bad French and Northern English if he had seen his friend. The waiter introduced me and I interpreted. Then the Englishman joined me at my table and asked me what I was doing there: I told him and returned the question.

'Oh, I'm working on the new steel works here. There's quite a lot of us on it.' He named two well-known British construction firms engaged on the project.

I mentioned that I thought the Tunisians seemed to have done pretty well for themselves since their independence.

'Yes, but from our point of view they're pretty hopeless. They know absolutely nothing about engineering. You try and get them to understand what you want done, and they haven't a clue.'

'How would they, after all, with no one to teach them?'

'Yes, I know, but you want to try working with them. It's enough to drive you crackers, I can tell you.'

When the Englishman had gone I relaxed in the warm sunshine with another beer or two. In this part of town most of the people wore European dress, and the girls, unencumbered by their white silk ha'iks, were able to exhibit their charms, which in many cases were remarkable, in the ordinary way. Dragging myself out of the pleasant lethargy that always overtakes me at pavement cafés in the sunshine, I struggled into my rucksack straps and strolled back to the Bourguiba statue in the étoile and found the Bizerta road. On this I selected a small grocery shop for a few odd stores, and at once fell into conversation with an extremely amiable, cultured man in European dress who insisted on buying me an orangeade and wanted to know about my travels. I illustrated these on my map and he showed me some other places of interest in Tunisia.

'I'm from Djerba, the island here off the coast. It's a funny thing, but you'll find that shopkeepers all over Tunisia come from Djerba.' Their representative there, who had just sold me a tin of sardines, grinned, indicating that he was no exception. I said that I would like to return to Tunisia some day to see the rest of it. 'I haven't even seen a camel yet.'

'There are plenty in the South, they are the cars of the desert.'

'Still, at least you have some wild animals here, don't you, in the Djebel Ischkeul?'

'Yes, wild boars, and suchlike.'

'Is that all? Someone told me yesterday there were lions.'

The cultured man smiled. 'You know 'Tartarin de Tarascon'? It's like that. You hunt rabbits and imagine they're lions. No, there's nothing in Djebel Ischkeul bigger than wild boars. Maybe a wolf or two and certainly foxes, but nothing much else.'

Sorry Gilani, no lions. The shopkeeper volunteered to fill my new water-can for me, and presently I was heading out of town along a suburban kind of road, with pleasant detached houses, to Tindja, which was a suburban kind of village. Admittedly, the road was still liberally strewn with Arabs and their animals, which lifted it out of the suburban kind of sterility encountered in, for instance, Sidcup.

From the bridge which crossed the connecting channel between the two lakes, I looked back at the dark mass of Djebel Ischkeul, velvety against the sinking sun, and the gleaming gold lake, its everyday muddiness transformed by the good fairy Vesper.

A couple of chaps passing by in a horse-drawn cart offered me a lift, and we shouted cheerfully to one another as I left the road and made camp in a field, overlooking the other, bigger, deeper lake, of Bizerta. It also overlooked the railway, and to supplement the two-toned hooters of the fine, up-to-date trains I had all the dogs of Tindja in concert with those of Menzel Bourguiba. As Gilani had observed, 'Everyone keeps a dog, and there are always far too many.' They could give even French, Corsican and Sardinian dogs lessons in sustained nocturnal cacophony.

They gave me the privilege of a wonderful, warm, clear-blue-skied day for Bizerta. To put it just right for time, allowing all afternoon for seeing the town, I hoped for a lift later in the morning, because there were sixteen kilometres to be covered and it

BIZERTA

would take all of three and a half hours. I passed over great sweeping expanses of cultivated land where a large number of ox-teams, horse-teams, mule-teams and horse-and-mule-teams were ploughing their prescribed squares. Here and there was a village or farmstead of gourbis, augmented by new whitewashed flat-roofed cabins. The lake, not far away, sparkled sea-blue, and over it swooped jet fighters from a nearby airfield. On the far shores Bizerta lay like an upset pail of milk.

I had eliminated six of the sixteen kilometres when my lift

arrived: as in Corisca and Sardinia, I never had to stop, look and wave a thumb at passing traffic, the lifts always came unsolicited, and uncannily often at precisely the right moment. This one, a small car with three young fellows already aboard, pulled up, apparently facing the wrong way. Puzzled, I queried this, because it was obvious which way I was going.

'No, we saw you just now, and turned round to pick you up. We're going back again now.' They all lived in Menzel Bourguiba, they said, and were going to work in Bizerta.

A wide, deep channel connects the Lake of Bizerta with the sea. On its shores are the wharves and docks of Bizerta, across it, ferries ply to the village on the other side. The latter, whose small towered mosque, white houses, and palm trees reflected in the placid water, I could see from where they put me down and drove off in the car. From the wharfside I strolled into Bizerta town, to a big square with tree-shaded gardens in the centre and great white arcaded buildings round the edges.

There are no signs now of the heavy damage the town suffered in the war of 1939–45: the modern part of it is neatly planned, clean, and full of new buildings, some in the old traditional Moorish style, some modern. The old part is no better and no worse than any other Arab quarter: whatever the smells are like there is always plenty of colour and life. The shoeshine boys wander, importuning, from table to table at the pavement cafés; the old men, bearded, swathed in cotton wrappings, cachabiya ragged at the edges, sandalled, ride past on their scraggy asses; workmen lope about in army greatcoat and red chechiya, and fat old women, conservative to the last, waddle slowly by in yards of white silk, their features completely obliterated by black veils; young lissom girls hurry home to lunch in ha'iks filmy enough to suggest that underneath they are dressed in jumper, skirt and nylons like any European shopgirl.

When I stopped in a street in the old town for a sketch of the great mosque, I was at once surrounded by a vast concourse of kids, all pushing and jostling and craning their necks to see what I was doing. They were just interested, and although most of their comments were in Arabic, I could pick out remarks like, 'He's a German.' 'No, American.' 'Look at his bag, he must be on a world tour.' 'What's he drawing?' 'Come and look, Ali, here's an American who's drawing the Mosque!'

Even when I finished the sketch, announced to the audience
that I was an Englishman, and left in the direction of the old port,
a great train of devotees followed, dogging every footstep, pausing when I paused.

The old port of Bizerta is beautiful. High, smooth crenellated
walls recall the days of Barbary pirates: the subtle, rhythmic
curves of fishing boats riding at the wharfside, reflecting liquidly
in the bright water, ring faint echoes of the corsairs' barques,
fast and rakish, that used to limp home, riddled with roundshot
but full of Europe's richest spoils and high-priced white slaves.

Just here, where old Daoud in his chechiya, reefer jacket and
Wellington boots was rolling out his nets to dry, could have been
the spot where the wretched slaves, manacled and shackled together, were pushed and prodded off the ships and assembled before being carted off to market and the end of their lives.

Yes, well, it may be all fancy, but you try wandering around on
a Bizerta quayside on a warm afternoon and see if you don't think
along those lines.

When I left Bizerta, by the ferry across the channel, one of the
small boys, with one eye filmed with the trachoma that afflicts far
too many of Tunisian children, still followed, even across the ferry.
Of course it was free, or he wouldn't have bothered, and I found
when we reached the Zarzouna shore that he was only trying to
beg a cigarette.

Chapter Nine

RETURN TO TUNIS

What turned out surprisingly to be the last camp of the whole trip was quite a good one, on a stretch of sand dune behind the sea wall, except that just the other side of the road there was a huge oil refinery, which made a frightful noise and went on doing it all night. Even then I might have got some sleep if it hadn't been for the early-morning shift, chatting cheerfully, going on duty at three in the morning. You can't have everything.

I had my usual spectator to watch me pack up camp and leave: someone always seemed to be on hand for that purpose. It was a dullish sort of day, and I wended my way towards the coastal cliffs and the hills just inland from them. The queerest thing was, on a stretch of road apparently devoid of any human habitation except for a couple of gourbis and an odd farmstead, an enormous long string of children, on their way to or from school. Where they came from, and where their school was, I have no idea. Perhaps it was all a mirage, and this was the kind of thing that happened to people who travelled in North Africa whether there was desert or not.

I came down to a town called Menzel Djemil and the edge of the lake, from which I could just see Menzel Bourguiba—again. The lake smelled rather nasty but as there was considerable activity in a fishery establishment built around a pier I imagine it was well stocked with fish hardy enough to compete with the sewage. Soon after lunch, when I was heading steadily south-east away from the lake, a green van stopped and its driver grinned and waved at me. He looked vaguely familiar but I couldn't place him until he reminded me that we had met just outside Chaouat on Friday when he was out on horseback, hunting. I had forgotten all about him, but now I remembered that I had thought he looked very fine, a sort of Valentino in modern dress, with rifle slung on his shoulder and a good bit of horseflesh between his knees. Now he was in a white overall, driving a laundry van, so he wasn't the Sheikh of Chaouat, after all. He told me that after he had made a call in Menzel Bourguiba, to which there was a turning I had just passed, he would be going back to Tunis, so why didn't I wait here for him and get a ride there? Well, it was a main road and apart from the ruins of Utica there wasn't much to see on the way, so I agreed, stipulating only that I would carry on and he could pick me up from wherever I happened to have got to by that time.

I started to climb up to the top of a ridge of hills leading in from the sea, and on a short cut from one hairpin to the next, encountered a ploughman who had just laboriously heaved his ancient wooden plough around at the end of a furrow. He stopped cursing his oxen and stared at me: for a twentieth-century ploughman, he was a sight. His ragged cachabiya was the same colour as the soil he was tilling, his chechiya was worn and greasy, faded to a pale pink, he was in Sardinian need of a shave and—soil, stones, trampling oxen and all, he was barefoot. He spoke only Arabic, but a gesture is enough for scrounging a cigarette. He probably didn't believe I had none, because everyone except a woman smokes in Tunisia.

I went through some South Downs kind of country, treeless but cultivated, with lovely sweeping curves of fields and hills and clean fresh sea-air. Then there was a great drop to a flat marshy plain, like Romney Marsh, with the sea in the distance and dotted white houses near the shore. The analogy with the famous Kent marshes was enhanced by the site, on a spur of low hill into the levels, of the old Phoenician port of Utica, high and dry and a good five miles from the sea, like a Cinque Port.

I was down on the levels by the time the hunter turned up with the van. He put my rucksack in the back with the laundry and I joined his mate, his uncle—an old grizzle-beard in a blue cachabiya and a chechiya bound with a strip of cotton cloth—and a little boy, in the front. It soon appeared that the hunter, who spoke good French in a gravelly voice, was as proud of the new Tunisia as the man I had met on the Menzel Bourguiba road. He told me a little of Bourguiba's finance scheme for the building of schools and colleges, the education of proper native-born technicians and engineers being a pressing need.

'Before,' he said, 'the French always brought in engineers from France or Italy whenever they wanted anything done. They never taught us anything. So we have to start from the beginning, but we are learning, slowly. I myself attend the Agricultural College, in Tunis.'

Handling the van, a Bedford oddly enough, with skill and phlegm, the hunter drove off the Tunis road along a dreadful mud-track, all potholes, half-bricks, lagoons and nightmares, to a slummy village of gourbis where his uncle lived. Uncle having been deposited, we skirted Tunis Airport and returned to civilization, past masses of new houses, all in the flat, square, nearly windowless style, and all whitewashed.

'Those,' said the hunter, 'have all been built since Independence. They are for the poorer people, and they have water, electricity, drains and so on.. Palaces, compared with the gourbis they used to live in.'

'So in time, the gourbis will disappear?'

'In time, yes.'

Ahead of us, high on a hill above the city, we could see the huge rectangular outline of the Tunis Hilton, a brand new acknowledgment that Tunis might well become a new honey-pot for the tourist flies. We stopped in a suburban street and parted. I had a long walk along a mile-long, double row of palm trees in the Avenue Mohammed V and reached the Avenue Habib Bourguiba and the City Centre.

I wanted to see Tunis properly, and be part of it for a while. I thought the most economical way of doing this would be to get a job and earn my keep for a couple of weeks, so after putting up at what I thought was a slightly better hotel than last time, in the Avenue de Paris, I went job-hunting.

To go round restaurants looking for work is not my favourite occupation; doing it in French isn't any easier. Being assured in each consecutive hotel, restaurant and eating-place that there were battalions of Tunisians waiting for a chance even to do the washing up, gave me the impression that I would have a better chance of earning a living by getting some brushes and joining the shoeshine brigade. After the first seven refusals I felt as if I was begging for a free meal; three hours later, after two suggestions that I should try the Hilton and one introductory note to its personnel manager, I had had enough. I decided, as a last resort, to try the Hilton the next morning and if that failed, to stay for a week on my own resources and leave by next Tuesday's boat.

There was a bar-restaurant next door to my hotel called Chez Paul. It was about the only eating-house in town I hadn't been to, asking for a job, and it was not too expensive, so I found a vacant place at one of its crowded tables, sat down and nearly went to sleep. I came to when my order arrived, and at the same time I became conscious that the people at the next table seemed to be talking about me. There was three men and a girl: two of the men black-haired, with indisputably Gallic features and mannerisms, the third bigger, bearded, with something Nordic about him, and the girl, although speaking French as fluently as the others, possessing the fair hair and fresh, rose-petal complexion seldom encountered south of the Isle of Wight. While pretending not to pay any attention I could hear them speculating whether I was American, French, Italian, German or God-knows-what-else, and without actually addressing me (as if they couldn't be sure in which language to do so) they clearly wanted me to settle the argument. I looked one of them in the eye and asked if he wished to speak with me.

'Yes, would you mind telling us what nationality you are?'

'I'm English.'

The girl squealed. 'There,' she said in the language I'm writing, 'I said you were. So'm I.'

'I thought you were.'

The bearded man laughed. 'I thought you were Belgian, Franklin said German and Thierry was sure you were Italian. We are all wrong, and Sue is right. How do you come here?'

I told them in a mixture of English and French and enjoyed their gay, friendly company until the time came when they got up and went, wishing me luck. I didn't expect ever to see them again.

The Personnel Manager of the Hilton, which I reached after a rain-drenched walk along the Avenue de Paris and up the hill, was extremely pleasant, spoke excellent English, and told me that as it was off season in Tunis he was actually cutting down his wage bill and certainly had no occasion to take on anyone else. I trudged back to town through the Parc Belvedere. Through the wire-netting of one of the Zoo enclosures, I saw the only camels I ever did see in Tunisia. One day I'll get round to seeing the other ninety-nine-hundredths of it, camels and all.

However, I *can* tell you something of Tunis and its people, because I spent some time looking at it, walking around it, and smelling it.

From the Parc Belvedere, which is mostly on the side of the Tunis Hilton's hill and apart from the Zoo, contains a casino, an eighteenth-century domed pavilion called the Koubba, and a fascinating assortment of semi-tropical vegetation, the Avenue de Paris runs straight in to join the Avenue Habib Bourguiba at right angles. Beyond the Place de l'Indépendence, with the mock-Moorish Cathedral on one side and the former Beys' palace, now the French Embassy, on the other, this becomes the Avenue de France and terminates quite abruptly, with the rest of the modern town, at the Porte de France. The principal purpose now of the Porte de France, once a battlemented gateway of the old city, is to provide shelter for at least two dozen shoe-polishing gentlemen, who set up their boxes and brushes early in the morning and stay there all day. Since half the population wear either sandals or blue and white canvas-and-rubber pumps, their multiplicity is hard to understand.

The Medina is the hub of old Tunis, the kernel from which all the rest has germinated. It is one of the most fascinating places I have ever seen. Its streets are twisting, narrow alleys, burrowing in between and under the houses—often they are vaulted tunnels—and intersecting in a baffling, maze-like complexity. Huge arched wooden doors, brightly painted and patterned with hundreds of black studs, lead into the mysterious depths of the ancient buildings; in the open streets high windows are veiled, like the women, not by black silk but black-painted wrought-iron grilles, in minute patterns that iron would never normally expect to find itself. In the streets, open and vaulted, are the souks: hundreds of tiny shops catering for the whole range of man's requirements. A whole street is devoted to one type of commodity: there is a street of silversmiths and goldsmiths, one of perfumiers, one of harness and saddle-makers, all leather-work patterned and beaded with gold and silver wire and coloured beads, a street of carpets and rugs, another of dyers and clothiers. Here is where you buy your chechiya and cachabiya, and embroidered jackets and slippers, your silks, tapestries, shawls and blankets. There are dozens of copper and brass-working shops, all clanging and banging away and turning out hundreds of pots and pans and relatively useless engraved plates and ashtrays and vases and

RUE DU RICHE,
TUNIS

coffee-pots for the tourists to buy. Any tourist, with money, could guarantee to spend the lot on the endless delights of the souks.

Of course, the souks are not just for tourists, because from the time I was there round to the Spring there are hardly any tourists. Mixed up with the trinket and souvenir shops there are second-hand shoe-shops, second-hand clothing shops like those I had seen in Mateur, and shops selling a vast array of cheap American clothing, mostly for women. Several streets are devoted also to food: fruit, vegetable, herb and spice shops, emitting a weird variety of aromatic flavours, stalls out in the open with fish and horrible blood-stained hunks of sheep, with flies buzzing around and who knows what lying in the gutter under your feet. There are hundreds of shops: they are all trying to make a living, and like the shoe-shiners of the Porte de France there is scarcely enough trade to stretch between a quarter of them. There is obvious poverty in the crowds jostling in the narrow streets: there are old men who could be mistaken for heaps of rubbish, one-eyed men, people of both sexes with hideously scarred faces, children with festering sores and lesions on faces, arms and legs, and eyes, grey with trachoma. Even so, in daylight at any rate, at no time did I get the Petticoat Lane feeling of having to swallow my wallet to avoid having it pinched: the shop-keepers I encountered were courteous and not over-persuasive, and although I incurred, by my dress (or perhaps my face: my clothes looked as if they had come out of the same second-hand store as everybody else's) a certain amount of staring and commentary, no one showed the least inclination to be anything but polite and affable. But that's the Tunisian Arabs for you: they have what the other Arabs call 'light-blood' and what the French call 'la douceur arabe'. In other words, they don't quarrel with you because you aren't one of them.

It is not easy to follow the architectural ramifications of the Medina, because half the time you are underneath them. Now and then you emerge and come face to face with the massive, soaring, embellished and spired tower of a mosque, like the candle-snuffer turret of a Rhenish castle. In one small square, a sort of vacuum with alleys leading off left, right and centre, I came upon a beautiful palace which accommodated the Museum of Dar Hussain. This was a collection of examples of Tunisian art, classic masterpieces in wood, metal and embroidery, tapestries, textiles and silks, centuries old and preserved carefully behind glass, with pale and faded colours but leaving no doubt of the genius of their design and execution. Quite a lot of the descriptive notices were in Arabic, which didn't help me particularly, but there was no denying the magic of early illuminated copies of the Koran, whether written in Arabic or any other set of runic symbols.

The palace itself was a joy to walk in: the small rooms lined a courtyard, and everywhere there was pattern and colour, intricately carved plaster ceilings and friezes, mosaics and arches and woodwork, and cool, withdrawn peace.

Tunis started life as a horrible little village called Thunes, built in between a series of shallow lagoons, and Carthage to it was as Pitt was to Addington and London was to Paddington. All good things come to an end, and Carthage was one of them. After the disaster known as the Hilalian invasion, when the rich lands of Tunisia were ravaged by the depredations of hordes of ignorant, barbarous nomads out of Egypt (they were sent on purpose by the Sultan as a punishment to Tunisia for disloyalty), the desirability of the coastal towns and ports was increased by the Tunisians' incapacity to defend them. Expeditionary Normans, Pisans and other rapacious Europeans occupied them and Tunisia was in an appalling mess. This was eventually sorted out by a Moroccan dynasty called the Hafsites, who succeeded in pacifying and uniting the country. Around the year A.D. 1230, they established their capital in Tunis, and it is from this period that some of the oldest buildings in the Medina date.

Rule by the Moorish kings came to an end just three hundred years later; a Turkish pirate called Kheireddine Barbarossa (which sounds to me like Red-beard) grabbed power in Tunisia and Algeria and exiled the last king. This was the era when the Emperor Charles V was concerning himself too closely with the business of half Europe: if the King of France had accepted Sampiero Corso's offer to remove him no doubt the same half of Europe would have been enormously grateful. So powerful a megalomaniac as the Emperor could not apparently let any Turkish pirate wave scimitars at him from the other side of the Mediterranean, so he sent in his Spanish armies to argue the point. This went on for forty years, if you can believe it, and in the end, in 1574, the Turks won. Piracy was established on a national footing and proved extremely profitable: Barbary corsairs became the curse of the Mediterranean and the delight of every subsequent writer on the subject.

Another adventurer happened in 1707. Hussein Ali had been a cavalry officer in Crete, but that didn't stop him directing a coup in Tunis which resulted in a dynasty of Beys which lasted until 1957, the date of Tunisian independence. The principal revenue of the Beys depended on piracy, and when this was terminated by French interference in the 1830's, they drifted so far into debt that they had to call in a European financial commission to untangle them and push them somwhere near solvency. Even then it was not until 1881 that France, through some careful engineering by their Prime Minister Jules Ferry and a crafty diplomat called Roustan, invaded the country and proclaimed it a protectorate. The Beys continued to succeed one another and reign impotently until the last one was gently and politely requested to leave.

When I had been in Tunis two days I happened on the second evening to be dining again in Chez Paul, having spent the day in Carthage (which I will talk about in the next chapter). To my pleasure I hadn't been there long before I was joined by Luc, the bearded Belgian, Franklin the Frenchman and Sue, the pretty fair-haired English girl. During the course of our conversation, which was lively, I happened to mention that I was not exactly delighted with my hotel. It was a seedy, miserable place, the bed had a malignant spring and prehensile sheets, my room was aired only by a skylight, and the reception clerk was a dark-visaged, ill-natured, insolent villain I called Black Mahmoud.

'Then we must rescue you from it at once,' said Luc. 'You can come and stay with me, I have a house in Carthage and a spare bed. You're welcome to it until you go home.'

I explained that, in response to an initial demand from Mahmoud, I had paid in advance—and had not asked for a receipt. This, as I later discovered, was an omission bordering on idiocy. Franklin began looking worried. 'I think,' he said, 'that you had better stay there tonight, and say nothing. Tomorrow, at lunch-time, I will meet you here and we will try and get this fellow to reimburse you. But it may be difficult.'

As we gathered outside Chez Paul, about to disperse, Sue

pointed to the front door of the hotel, next door. 'Is that the place?'

'Unfortunately, yes.'

'It's really bad, is it?'

'Atrocious,' I said.

At midday the following day I met Franklin and Luc in Chez Paul; we demolished a couple of beers, accompanied by the usual gratuitous dishes of little squids, fried rouget fish, winkles and so on, then Franklin said, 'Come on, let's go.'

Black Mahmoud was in his den, behind the reception desk, enveloped in a brown cachabiya. Franklin shook hands with him and explained that due to unforeseen circumstances I was obliged suddenly to leave the hotel, and would be grateful if he would return the 2,400 millims, at 600 per night, that I had paid in advance for the next four days. Mahmoud, knave that he was, contrived to look baffled. How could he owe me 2,400, he said, when I had only paid five hundred a night? Look, here it was in the register: paid in advance for seven days, at five hundred per night, three and a half dinars. Possibly, said Franklin cautiously, there had been a mistake. Monsieur was positive that he had paid six hundred per night, but in any case since he wished to leave he must be reimbursed at once.

Blandly Mahmoud closed his register. 'No, that is impossible. I cannot pay out any money, I have just banked the week's takings. You will have to wait until the Patron comes, this evening.'

Franklin turned to me. 'We'll have to do as he says. It's the Patron we must see, to get any money back at all. And I have a feeling that's not going to be easy.'

'This animal,' I said, considerably incensed, 'is a thief. The Patron owes me two dinars, all right, but he owes me the seven hundred millims he has pocketed for himself!'

'I know, but it is his word against yours, and no proof. We must go very, very gently, or we'll get nothing. Let me do the talking.'

At seven-thirty in the evening Franklin and I returned to the attack. The Patron, whom I had never seen before, turned out to be a youngish, small man, pale and bespectacled. Franklin approached the situation with consummate diplomacy and handshakes all round, mentioned my difficulty and asked for the reimbursement of the two dinars which, according to the register, were due to me. This is ridiculous, I thought, it should be automatic if a guest decides to leave early, he gets his money back. Quite apart from the reception clerk doing me out of ten bob.

Yielding at last under the persuasive pressure of Franklin's entreaties, which included a hint that failure to reimburse customers would be extremely bad publicity for Tunis, the Patron reluctantly unlocked a tin money-box and handed over two dinars. The question of the other seven hundred appropriated by Mahmoud, who was hovering in the background, came up, and was rejected. 'But he,' I said, butting in at last, 'is a thief. He has stolen this money from me, and you know it.'

The Patron shrugged his shoulders indifferently. As Franklin had forecast, without proof of Mahmoud's duplicity he was prepared to yield nothing more. I collected my kit from that dreary little room upstairs and we left.

In Chez Paul, over a comforting Celtia beer (a Tunisian brand which is better than anything France has brewed) Franklin explained to me, at length, and twice since I failed to understand the first time (we spoke entirely in French because he knew no English) the reason why the Patron was so reluctant to pay back the money.

'You see, the Patron, he with the spectacles, knows very well that it is a rotten hotel. He also knows that he in the cachabiya is a thief. He knows that the hotel is so bad that it wouldn't matter either way if the publicity, resulting from his refusal to reimburse you, was adverse. All he is after is whatever small income he can possibly get from it, before it is obliged to close down. If I had not persuaded him as gently as I did, he would not have paid you anything back at all. As it is, you've only lost the seven hundred millims, which—'

'I know,' I smiled ruefully, 'which was my fault anyway. But you see this is the first time, in travels in several different parts of Europe—I admit this is my first experience of North Africa—that I have encountered the slightest suspicion of dishonesty in a hotelier. I should have asked for a receipt, and if I had Mahmoud would probably have climbed down and said he'd made a mistake over the price of the room or something. But I didn't, and I should think plenty of other people would make the same mistake. Don't you think Tunis ought to try and clean up

these wretched third-class hotels, if they want to encourage tourists?'

'Certainly, and no doubt they will, in time. The point is, that if you know, you don't have to go to them at all.'

'What do you mean?'

'Well,' Franklin said, 'the first class hotels, like the Majestic, and Claridge, are about half as expensive as their equivalent in Europe, and if you can stay in them as cheaply as that, why bother about these seedy old places at all?'

As he said, if you know in advance, you can avoid the pitfalls. If you don't know, down you go.

Chapter Ten

CARTHAGE

The train to Carthage runs along one of the embankments of the ship canal, between the two parts of the Lake of Tunis. After La Goulette, at the entrance to the canal, begins a long sprawl of houses and villas bearing recognisable signs of middle and upper class affluence, stretching all along the side of the gulf as far as Sidi-bou-Saïd on the point. In the course of five miles the train stops at a dozen stations, four or five of which say they are part of Carthage: Salammbo, Byrsa, Annibal, Amilcar and so on. I left the train at Carthage-Byrsa, and started looking for antiquities.

There are plenty of relics of ancient masonry scattered about Carthage, but they speak far more of the grandeur that was Rome than the same category previously enjoyed by Carthage. The insistence of the implacable Cato that Carthage must be destroyed eventually resulted in just that: hardly two stones were left standing, and when the Romans decided to reconstruct the place they had to start entirely from scratch. Today's ruins, therefore, are Roman ruins. Punic relics do exist, but they consist mostly of sarcophagi, tombstones, jugs, pots, coins and similar everyday, functional objects: there is very little evidence of the legendary Punic art.

The first ruins I came to were those of a theatre, one of those semi-circular auditoria with tiers of seats and the stub-ends of columns to show where the stage, wings and dressing-rooms had been. It was in a dilapidated condition and not very exciting, but just over the hill towards the sea there was what looked like High Street, Carthage, wide, paved and guttered, and the low ground-floor walls of most of its shops and houses. Foliated columns were everywhere, lining the streets and marking the doorways, and in the centre one of the larger houses, with a fine terrace overlooking the Gulf, had been resuscitated, roofed and outfitted as an Antiquarium. This cost fifty millims to get into, and before even I reached it I had been accosted by three boys of varying sizes

CARTHAGE

RLL

and ages, who wanted to act as guides and also to sell me various
odd coins and pieces of pottery they had found, acquired or
nicked. One of them accompanied me into the museum and
started gratuitously to tell me that this was a bust of Hannibal and
that was a Punic sarcophagus and the other was a Byzantine

medallion, despite the fact that they were all marked quite clearly in both French and Arabic and I could see for myself. I pointed this out, and added that my happiness would not be irretrievably wrecked nor my day spoilt if he were to deprive me of his company. This cut no ice at all, so I told him to get out, and eventually he did—for a while.

The Antiquarium, although small, was full of such Punic, Roman and Byzantine relics as had not been filched already and taken to the much larger national museum at Le Bardo, in the old Beylical Palace, not to mention the Louvre and no doubt the British Museum too. Outside on the terrace, among a large collection of columns, coffin-lids and armless, headless busts and statues, were some particularly fine mosaics, showing well-proportioned fishes, and hunting scenes with tigers and leopards spotted and striped as accurately as illustrations in a Sunday paper colour-supplement. The sun at that moment happened to be shining, and the first whiff of old Carthage came floating into the atmosphere; the Gulf lay shining and tranquil beyond the palm trees on the shore (ignoring the flat roofs of the modern houses beside it) and the dark mountains on the other side were just as Hannibal, who spent most of his life in Spain, probably hardly ever saw them.

Still, thousands of lesser Carthaginians undoubtedly did see them, and two modern Carthaginians, not bothering about them at all, were still doing their best to sell me some coins and Hannibal's-head lamps which they claimed were absolutely genuine. My nephew is an enthusiastically pro-Carthaginian antiquarian, so for his benefit I sat down on a two-thousand-year-old wall with the two boys and began a prolonged haggling session for ownership of the less unlikely of their relics. Later, in a conversation with Sue, I mentioned that I had bought from the local lads a couple of Punic lamps.

'Oh,' she said, 'not the one with Hannibal's head, and his beard in three forks with holes in for the burners? Everybody buys those. Either the Carthaginians mass-produced the things, or those boys do in their back yards. Still, they are rather nice, and they could just as well be genuine as not, and they do come from Carthage itself, so why not?'

Actually, they quite probably are genuine, because the Carthaginians did make large numbers of such ordinary articles: if you dug up London in a couple of thousand years' time, you would probably find hundreds of cups and saucers, and beer-mugs, and cigarette lighters and so on. They wouldn't be any more valuable than my Punic lamps (which are worth no more than I paid for them—and probably less) but they would still be genuine relics. But I wonder how many tourists to Cartharge have bought these things, and more particularly Roman and Byzantine coins, thinking they have made a fantastic bargain, and found as I did when I took my coins to a numismatist at home that they are worthless? I mention this point as a mild warning to anyone who thinks he has made a fortune by paying a few hundred millims to a small boy in old Carthage for something of which 'the lad obviously had no idea of the real value'. Who's kidding who?

Next I found a small temple, on the way up to the hill of Byrsa. It had most of its tall, graceful columns standing, but no walls or roof. From the top of the hill, near the Cathedral, I could see in the plain behind the coastal hills the grey shapes of further parts of Roman Carthage. I could also see the approach of what was clearly going to be a heavy rainstorm. The Cathedral of Saint-Louis, is of course modern, and was built in a ghastly mock-Moorish style with minarets, cupolas and columns, and is in a noticeably shabby condition. It was locked, so I couldn't even shelter in it from the rain. It struck me that for a minority religion in this country, a Christian church of this size, so manifestly too big for its congregation, was not likely to earn much in the way of respect from the followers of Mohammed. Still, a saint is a saint, and France's saint-king did honour the place by dying here, after all.

It was in 1270, and King Louis IX, who was indeed a saintly and wise king but a rotten soldier, was on his way to one Crusade too many. He and his court camped, for a moment of archaeological reminiscence, among the ruins of Carthage, before laying seige to Tunis. Louis naïvely maintained that he had only to show his saintly face to the Mohammedan King of Tunis for that gentleman, and all his people, to fall down in abject contrition and offer themselves for conversion to Christianity. Half France was along for the fighting and the spoils, and even our Edward, Prince of Wales, who later became King Edward I, was there with a small force. But provisioning for army, princes, kings and all was deplorably inadequate, and the outcome of it was that most of the Crusaders went down with one kind of fever or another, and disease being no respecter of rank or position the King was among them. He was an old man and incapable of withstanding such severe physical delibility: in Carthage he died.

Legend tells queer tales. The full irony of the situation is that Holy Saint Louis did not die after all: instead he was converted to Islam and became a marabout, a Moslem saint! And Sidi-bou-Saïd is named after him. Well, that's the story the Tunisians tell, anyway.

In the nineteenth century the French consul bought the hill of Byrsa from the Bey of Tunis and had a memorial tomb built for

Thermal Baths, Carthage

Saint Louis. Later, in the early years of the protectoracy, the vast and tasteless cathedral was built.

On the southern slope of the hill of Byrsa, below the cathedral, I found, in addition to a fine cloud-hung prospect of the lakes, the Gulf, and Tunis itself, some peculiar stalagmitic remains of Byzantine buildings with fragments, according to the notice-board, of Punic construction. As to which was which, the notice was not so explicit, nor was it easy to make head or tail of the tumbled heaps of stone, clay and rock that comprised the ruins. If you go to see this particular part of Carthage, take an archaeologist with you.

The weather now having erupted I spent the rest of the afternoon dodging showers of rain. Shelter from them, after a series of trees along the road down from Byrsa, took the form of enormous slabs of Roman masonry in the Antonine Thermal Baths. These had been built, as substantially as the Romans knew how, on the

sea shore, and had obviously been the biggest and best and probably the most up-to-date of all thermal baths of the age. Huge
vaulted bath-houses were connected by walks, cloisters, and a
square or meeting place, the whole covering several acres and containing hundreds of tons of original two-thousand-year-old building material. Particularly fine capitals, heads and other sculpture
had been collected in the first bath-house, along with inscriptions
in that close-written upright style with the words all running into
one another, that the Romans chose to adopt for our ultimate
confusion. Modern inscriptions by the Tunisian Historic Monu-
ments Department were neither frequent nor obtrusive, but sure
as fate there just had to be an engraved tablet set in the biggest
chunk of masonry in the square, saying 'From Carthage, Mis-
souri, to Carthage, Tunis'. There is only one Carthage, just as
there is only one Paris and only one London, and should not be
mentioned in the same breath with any modern shantytown with
a borrowed name.

Rising uphill from the Baths are beautiful gardens, intersected
with ancient streets and avenues and set about with numbers of
house foundations, quantities of grave-stones and sarcophagi,
scores of perpetually brightly-coloured mosaics, and several
temples and chapels. Even then, in December, the gardens glowed
with glorious reds and purples: flowers, shrubs and trees all contributing. Christian Carthage was represented here, by a tiny
underground chapel which had been discovered in Saida, a few
miles away, and transferred wholesale, and by the floor and
symmetric columns of a Byzantine basilica. Christianity in Roman
Carthage was represented by some of the staunchest, most in-
defatigable, fervid and dedicated martyrs of the lot. One or two
might seem to have been rather overdoing it, so insistent they
were on being martyred, but they probably converted as many
waverers to the Faith as a Billy Graham Crusade.

There are plenty more Roman ruins in Carthage: there is the
Amphitheatre, the Forum and sundry other villas, and there is
also another Byzantine basilica. But the old, aboriginal Carthage
is just a glorious memory.

Tradition has it that Carthage was founded in the year 814 B.C.
Quite how tradition arrives at this exact date, considering the
almost total lack of reliable information relevant to the momen-
tous occasion, is not certain. Tradition might well have added that

it was on a wet Tuesday afternoon in late September, it would make just as much sense. Tradition also maintains that the city was founded by Dido, the widowed daughter of the King of Tyre, who happened to have landed there after a long voyage from her home port. Tradition here is backed up by fact, because certainly the founders were Phoenicians, and certainly it was they who called their new trading emporium Kart Hadasht, which means the New City, and the nearest the Romans could get to saying that was Carthago. But the existence of Queen Dido, amorous dalliance with Aeneas, the escaping Trojan, and all, remains apocryphal. Still, if we accept Aeneas, and Odysseus, why not Dido? Let's have our legends, they make better stories than plain Phoenician commerce, however enterprising.

When Tyre and Sidon succumbed to the all-conquering Alexander the Great (or Alexander the Mediocre, as someone unkindly described the Hollywood film made about him) the wealthier denizens of those cities got away in great haste to North Africa, where their interests were mainly vested. This was to the advantage of the trading towns and particularly Carthage, which enjoyed the combination of an easily defensible position with a fertile and productive hinterland. Carthage thereafter built the biggest ships, sponsored the best sailors and opened up the most lucrative trading channels. In these very early times Carthage had a financial and economic system the envy of the civilised world: while the Romans were still wrestling with little bits of metal, Carthage had bank-notes, made of leather. Following the sound precept of exploiting military conquests by taxing new colonies for all they were worth, Carthage had plenty of money in the bank to back the notes, which found favour all round the Mediterranean. So there was Carthage, a city on the make, seeking and finding prosperity in all parts of the known world and even some parts of the unknown world: voyages of discovery down the African coast were not unheard of. Punic, or Phoenic Carthage, was having its day.

Energy is the commodity most necessary for promulgating and maintaining an empire, and once that declines, through the usual processes of degeneration through affluence and delegation of effort, it is time for another bull to lead the herd. The young bull with more energy than the old was Rome.

Carthaginian power was still paramount, although Cartha-

ginian morals were already deplorable, when Rome started to become a serious challenge to their supremacy.. One of the least en-
dearing Carthaginian customs was the sacrifice of babies, which
they threw into a fire in order to propitiate their god Baal-
Haman, while their mothers were supposed to look on unmoved.
It is said on occasion nearly three hundred babies a day were mur-
dered in this inconceivably inhuman fashion. With this kind of
thing in mind, one can bear with greater fortitude and less trouble
to the emotions the tragedy of the fall of Punic Carthage.

Three wars, over a period of a hundred years, between Carthage and Rome, achieved this cataclysm, and it is a mark of the
energy of the Romans that they survived some pretty drastic dis-
asters and came out on top. The best known of the wars is the
middle one, in which Hannibal, son of Hamilcar Barca, took an
army in which he was almost the only Carthaginian, from Spain
where he lived most of his life (the town is still called Cartagena)
across southern France, over the Alps and down into Italy, elephants and all. He beat the Romans resoundingly in four classic
battles, and could have taken Rome when it was undefended
bar a scratch force of disorganised irregulars. But he hesitated,
waited for reinforcements from Carthage which Carthage,
having a short-sighted, self-centred inclination to cling to every
penny and every elephant in its possession, refused to send him,
and in the end marched the other way. So did Carthage: by denying Hannibal the support he deserved, they missed the opportunity of smashing Rome and ending the contention over who was
boss in the Mediterranean. Rome survived, Publius Cornelius
Scipio took an army to Tunisia, and at Zama, in 202 B.C., fifty
miles south-west of Carthage, Hannibal and the Carthaginians
were beaten in battle.

The Third Punic War merely finished the job: Carthage was
already beaten and deprived of her supremacy. The ultimate
destruction of the city was due to premeditated vindictiveness on
the part of the Romans, headed by Cato, who kept insisting that
Carthage should be destroyed, come what may. The excuse was
provided by an attack by the exasperated Carthaginians on King
Massinissa of Numidia, an ally of Rome who repeatedly ravaged
and plundered Carthaginian properties. With righteous indignation the Romans demanded excessive and extortionate ransoms
from the Carthaginians, in the form of hundreds of babies from

the best families, all the city's arms, ships, and most of its harvest. Carthage complied: the bloodthirsty Romans were still not satisfied, they wanted Carthage destroyed, and destroyed it must be, whether justifiably or not. A descendant of Scipio led an army and lay siege to the town. It lasted three years, and Carthage resisted to the very last. When every building was in flames and ninety per cent of the population killed, Scipio asked the Senate in Rome if he could stop the slaughter. No: Carthage must be destroyed.

Carthage was burned to the ground, broken up, ploughed under. Its few survivors were sold into the African slave markets. A whole city and five hundred thousand people had ceased to exist.

But a hundred years later a New City was founded, by Julius Caesar, one of the colonies that thoughtful man established for his veteran legionaries: towns in all parts of the empire populated by loyal ex-soldiers were going to be much more reliable than towns full of rebellious locals. Quickly the massive buildings rose about the old site, and in quite a short time Carthage was a flourishing port again—a whole-heartedly Roman port. When the empire split in two, Carthage came under the rule of Byzantium, whose loose and inept grip slipped when the Vandals came across the ditch from Europe and appropriated it, in A.D. 435. In 534 Byzantium, recovering somewhat, took it back from them, but Byzantine rule never was remarkable for any inspired hold on its subject peoples, or any vigorous defence against invaders. In the middle of the seventh century the Arabs arrived and the Byzantines left; far from going out in a blaze of glory like Punic Carthage, Byzantine Carthage was merely abandoned, and used as a convenient stone-quarry for the building, to Arab taste, of Tunis. And so much for Carthage, until France and the railway came.

Luc's house was in the road running alongside the railway, near Carthage-Annibal station. It was a small house, sparsely furnished, but Luc had all his meals in Tunis and only used the house, which he had rented for the winter, to sleep in. But across the railway it had a prospect of the Gulf, and the mountains on its far side, and in the back garden there were orange trees. I had never before picked an orange off a tree.

We spent most of the weekend sauntering around Tunis, up the Avenue Habib Bourguiba and the Avenue de Paris, dining in sundry restaurants, drinking beer and coffee in a remarkably wide variety of bars, meeting friends—Franklin in Chez Paul, Sue in the Café de Paris and an apparently unlimited supply of Luc's other friends and acquaintances—and went to the pictures on Saturday afternoon. The sound was bad, and most of the audience consisted of children, for whom the film was highly unsuitable. They spent the whole time running up and down the aisles and making an incredible noise. 'Why on earth do they come?' I asked.

Luc shrugged. 'It's Saturday afternoon, so they go to the pictures.' But we had to leave: neither of us could understand what was being said on the screen.

We located Franklin again in Chez Paul to find out the address of a party to which we had been invited, and went there, the top flat of a large block off the Avenue de Paris. There were four other Belgians, two Americans and three Tunisian girls, and at about one o'clock in the morning, Franklin and Thierry turned up. There was plenty to eat, plenty to drink and plenty of talk; there was dancing and singing, wine and whisky. My recollection of getting back to Carthage, at some weird hour of the morning, is hazy in the extreme, and when I woke up I discovered that I was still fully clothed. It was a grand party.

On Monday, at lunch, we fortunately ran into René, the owner of the flat, and were able to apologise; Erik had also been present and we found ourselves invited to another party that night at his house in Le Kram. Sue, who was lunching with us on the strength of a birthday, was included in the invitation.

Weekends in Tunis, Luc observed, were too dead to be believed. There were a number of cinemas, mostly showing very bad films, and nothing much else (at that time of the year, anyway). The people just strolled in the streets, which in the rain was not too entertaining for them. 'For most of them,' Luc said, 'it's their weekend pleasure, just walking in the avenues. They can't afford anything else.'

Having spent nearly all Sunday afternoon in a diversity of bars and cafés, we went in the evening to Sidi-bou-Saïd. By that time it had not only stopped raining but the evening was soft, warm and starry, and Sidi-bou-Saïd, the village on the cliffs beyond Carthage, was enchanting.

Compared with all the other Arab villages I had seen, Sidi-bou-

SIDI - BOU - SAÏD

Saïd was an architectural gem. The houses were large, tall and substantial, and exuded the aura of wealth. Wickets in the great wooden, sky-blue-painted, black-studded doors stood open and we caught glimpses of richly carpeted, cool, clean, tasteful interiors. Elaborate oriel windows, latticed and grilled in sky-blue paint and black wrought-iron, overhung the cobbled streets.

'Those,' said Luc, 'are called mesharabiyahs. The ladies can sit up there and see everything that's going on in the street without being seen themselves.'

We walked about the narrow, quiet streets, lit by occasional old-fashioned lamps, walked up flights of worn stone steps to other streets, and bought some hot doughnuts called bombaloni from a little shop where they were cooking them to order. We wiped away the last of the sugar and strolled out past the cemetery to a point overlooking the smooth black sea. We were on the furthest promontory of the cliffs, before the shore-line swept back to La Marsa and the sand-dunes of Gammarth. It was quiet, relaxing, peaceful, the air full of mingling sweet scents and the suggestion of pity that we had missed an opportunity, on such a night, by coming here without feminine company.

> 'In such a night
> Stood Dido with a willow in her hand
> Upon the wild sea-banks, and waft her love
> To come again to Carthage.'

We made our way back to the centre of the village, to the little square at the head of the main street, and mounted the stone steps to the rounded doorway of the old café. It was a large room, pillared and painted in stripes and designs; there were very few tables and chairs, the customers were to remove their shoes and squat on a large stone dais, covered with rush mats. There they could converse with their friends, play cards, and drink scented tea and thick Turkish coffee. Around the walls were hanging a number of exquisitely wrought bird-cages, painted white: their inmates cheeped and chattered in competition with that monotonous, yet evocative Arab music from the radio. It was a café 'plus arabe que les Arabes' but it was patronised by locals of European and Jewish extraction as much as Arabs. In Tunisia there is courtesy to all-comers, even tourists.

'Plenty of dinars in this place, Luc,' I observed, as we watched a party of young men and girls enter and spread themselves over one of the platforms, lining up their shoes on the floor.

'Yes, that's because it's the home of a lot of doctors, lawyers and so on, the professional class of Tunis. Foreigners, too, officials from all the various embassies, with big salaries, have bought these fine old houses. And rich Tunisians, Jew and Arab merchants, too.'

It is not a coincidence that Sidi-bou-Saïd is so aesthetically pleasing: it is a nostalgic reconstruction of past Moorish glories in Andalusia. When the Spaniards finally drove the Moors out of their country, a colony of them, a mixture of Jews and Arabs, made their home in Sidi-bou-Saïd. The village they built is a tangible memory, a poignant lament for their beautiful homes in Spain.

Shopping in the Tunis souks is an entertaining business. The customer is of course not expected to pay the price he is first asked, unless he is a complete idiot, and the purchase of a large article, like a cachabiya, is more of a social occasion than a commercial transaction. An Englishman, and more particularly an American, is at an immediate disadvantage, because of the Tunisian assumption that anyone from those countries is rich. Even when I indicated the great hole that had by this time appeared in my trouser-leg, they refused to believe that I could not afford to buy the whole shop if I chose to. I still fancied myself in a cachabiya, which seemed to me to be the ideal garment in which to weather the normal English winter, and having settled on the one I wanted had a half-hour struggle with the shopkeeper and his young lad (who brought me a cup of coffee at half time) to beat them down to something like a reasonable price. They started at twelve dinars. I started at four. Eventually they capitulated at seven, and I discovered later that the proper price for a cachabiya of that quality (it is a good one, of thick camel-wool) is five.

In another shop, where I wished to buy several small objects but hesitated to do so because the man there was asking a dinar here and eight hundred millims there, in desperation he drew up a list, knocking off two or three hundred in each case, and arriving at what was probably a bit nearer the correct price. To show my appreciation of this incredible generosity I gave the man some British stamps and coins I still had in my possession, as souvenirs, and we had a long chat about affairs in Tunisia. Of the

President, the man said, 'Bourguiba is more than a president to us, he is more like a father to us all. He has given us hope and self-respect, and we look up to him.'

I told Luc about this later, and mentioned that I had heard the same deference to the President from a number of sources.

'Yes,' he said, 'but you've only heard the common people's point of view. The professional classes are not nearly so keen on him, because of his strict financial restrictions. It's impossible to get money out of this country, so no one can invest in possibly lucrative foreign markets. The dinar is sacrosanct: tourists can come and spend their money, but if they stay as residents for any length of time and start earning money, they aren't tourists any more and can't get it out. Listen, there's a joke about Bourguiba going round.' We were in Chez Paul at the time. 'I'd better not say Bourguiba too often in case someone hears and we get thrown out: I'll say B.

'B. dies and goes to Heaven. It's extremely pleasant there, but after a while he finds life very dull. He goes to God and says, "Can't I go somewhere else for a while? I'm bored here." And God says, "All right, I'll give you a visa to go down to Purgatory for a week, and if that's still too dull, to Hell for another week." So B. goes to Purgatory, and it's quite jolly there, beer and singing and so on, but that palls after a week and B. uses the other half of his visa and goes on down to Hell. There it's very lively, cards, and roulette, and whisky, and women, and B. has a whale of a time. At the end of the week his visa expires and he has to go back to Heaven.

'When he gets back, he goes to God and says, "Can't I stay permanently in Hell, it's so much fun there?" And God says, "Yes, I'll give you a permit to stay as long as you like." So B. goes back to Hell and for a while life is great. But after two or three months he can't stand it any more, he really hates it, and longs for the peace and quiet of Heaven again. So he goes up to the Pearly Gates and asks Saint Peter if he can come back in.

'Saint Peter looks at the date B.'s permit was issued. "No," he says, "you can't come back. It was all right while you were just a visitor down there, but now you're a resident and you'll have to stay there!"'

On the deck of the *Ville de Marseille*, as she slipped smoothly through the calm Mediterranean night past the rocky south-western shores of Sardinia, I had conversation with a Tunisian gentleman, and he told me a great deal about the Tunisian social structure.

'In Tunisia,' he said, 'there are four classes. Let us call them A, B, C and D. First, A, there is the capitalist class, and there are more of them than you might think. Then, B, comes the professional class, all well-educated—abroad. C is the middle class: clerks, shop-keepers and farmers, with a small education. Lastly, D is the common people, with no education and even less money.

'Now Habib Bourguiba had tried to raise the living standards of C and D by borrowing from A and B and not permitting them to invest money or buy anything outside Tunisia. The dinar is protected at all cost. The money is used to build factories, schools and colleges, and new houses to replace the gourbis. Hence Bourguiba is popular with C and D and not with A and B. To add to this, he has insisted on absolute equality: where, "avant", no Tunisians were allowed the rich, plushy jobs, or to stay in the best hotels, or even drink in the best bars, now anyone has the right to do anything.

'You probably noticed the enormous number of poor people hanging around the streets of Tunis? I'll tell you the reason for that. It happens that a country man gets fed up with scratching a living in the primitive country life—and that can be really primitive, I can tell you—so he comes to town. At once he is vastly impressed with the bright lights and the big buildings, and he thinks it's Heaven. He and his wife spend far too much on gaudy American clothes in the souks, and both of them try to get work to make up for it. Then they find that Tunis is full of thousands of simple souls like them, all with the same object in mind: to live in the flashy, colourful, exciting city. The result is that the woman does domestic work for a pittance, and the man does either nothing at all, or joins the already superfluous numbers of shoe-cleaners.'

On my last evening in North Africa, Luc, Franklin and I went to Le Kram, which is a residential suburb on the coast between La Goulette and Carthage. The party consisted mainly of Belgians, all working in Tunis, with their wives: to Luc's guitar we sang—or rather, they sang, a succession of Flemish folk-songs, boisterous affairs that Franklin and I could not follow. Latish, from another party, Sue turned up, looking lovely in blue; in the small hours we returned her, by someone's car, to Tunis. At two-thirty I wrapped myself in my new cachabiya and lay down on the divan in Luc's house in Carthage. Three hours later I was up again and leaving, shaking hands with Luc and thanking him yet again, to catch the train to the port of Tunis.

At the port I met Roy Lewis again, my fellow-bum from Birmingham. From the deck of the *Ville de Marseille* we watched a fantastic African sunrise: the sun, blazing over the Cap Bon hills on the eastern side of the Gulf, painted the water red and gold, the wispy mist under the hills pale pastel mauve, the sky and the clouds the colours Turner saw in his skies and clouds; it painted the massed houses, towers and mosques of the town and the flamingoes—yes, they were flamingoes—on the lake, a perfect, rosy, strawberry-ice pink.

The *Ville de Marseille* sailed: along the five miles of the ship-canal, out into the Gulf, past La Goulette, Le Kram, Carthage, Sidi-bou-Saïd, out to sea.

It took me five nightmare days to hitch-hike home from Marseille, and Roy Lewis had an even worse journey: but that is another story.